Appletree Guides

IRISH FAMILY NAMES

IDA GREHAN

Contents

First published and printed by
The Appletree Press Ltd
7 James Street South
Belfast BT2 8DL
1985

9 8 7 6 5

Illustrations by Karen Bailey

British Library Cataloguing in Publication Data
Grehan, Ida
Irish family names.
1. Names, Personal — Ireland
I. Title   929.4'2'09415   CS2415

ISBN 0-86281-133-3

Introduction

The Irish are a remarkably literary people. Writing — or talking about writing — is one of their main industries. Their intense interest in genealogy could be said to have been their first step along the road to literature. Pedigrees are about people. From earliest days the Irish could recite the descent of their families from ancient kings and chieftains. Reciting the litany of names provided the poets and the musicians with an endless flow of stories as heroic characters were recalled; Malachy who lost his collar of gold; Cormac MacCarthy who built the miniature church on the Rock of Cashel; Cearbhal, the warlike, Brian Boru's swordsman, who gave his name to the O Carrolls; Clerieach, Clark, progenitor of the O Clearys who helped compile the *Annals of the Four Masters* with its invaluable genealogical information.

The hewers of wood and drawers of water who had no names assumed the surnames of their chieftains — hence the importance of an authenticated pedigree.

Nicknames became respectable. Cruitín (hunchback) became MacCurtin. Dochartaigh meant 'obstructive' which, at one time, the O Dohertys were. The Norsemen the natives dubbed Dubhgall (dark stranger), are now the numerous Doyles. MacNamara, from the Irish which means 'hound of the sea', aptly described this sept on the seacoast of Clare. Ceallachain, meaning 'strife', probably described an earlier breed of O Callaghans. Conchobhair, 'hero' or 'champion', suited the Connacht O Connors who were High Kings of Ireland. The O Donnells of Tyrconnell, whose name means 'world mighty', are descendants of King Niall of the Nine Hostages, progenitor of many leading families, including the O Neills.

In Austria, where the Irish were very early missionaries, they are still known as Scots, a name they got from the Romans when they raided Britain from Ireland.

Hereditary surnames came spontaneously and compartatively early to Ireland — between the 10th and the 11th centuries. The prefix Mac meant 'son of', while O could signify either grandson, or earlier ancestor. Fitz, from the French 'fils', also meant 'son of'. A girl used Ni before her father's name, while her mother prefixed Ban.

During the centuries when the Irish and their Catholic religion were suppressed they were forced to drop these prefixes and to translate their names into English, which has led to some confusion such as MacAodhagain (Egan) becoming Keegan, or MacMathghamhna (MacMahon) becoming Vaughan, and many more.

Beginning with the Celts from Spain and then the Vikings who swept down from Scandinavia in their long boats to raid the coast, pillage the monasteries and found cities, Ireland absorbed a diversity of settlers. Unfortunately the Romans never got to Ireland. The Normans made the greatest impact with their fine stone buildings and their continental vitality and connections. Their names have long since become accepted as Irish. What Dillon, or Power, or FitzGerald would think he was anything other?

The sept, rather than the clan, was the Irish dynastic system. It comprised a group whose immediate ancestors had a common name and lived in the same locality. Chieftaincies were not hereditary — which often led to bloodshed or putting out of eyes: a maimed chieftain would not be acceptable.

With the easing of the discriminatory laws against the native Irish and a growing confidence in their own individuality, the prefix Mac and O began to be resumed in the late 19th century.

To trace a family back 1,000 years is to see the panorama of Irish history. To trace several families is to learn world history. Driven abroad by sword or famine the Irish fought on every side on battlefields in Europe, Russia and America north and south. They spread the gospel, filled high legal and political office, developed countries and commerce. They were journalists, dramatists, actors and labourers on the railroads and in the mines. Only recently have they begun to surface on an international level in music and painting, arts difficult for a suppressed people to follow.

There are millions more Irish men and women in Britain and the Americas, Australia, Argentina and Canada, than there are in Ireland. Eighty out of a possible 3,500 names is a modest offering. It is attempted in the hope of revealing a versatile race and giving a factual and balanced story of the island of Ireland through the vicissitudes of its leading families.

The Irish Genealogical Office which was established in 1552 has its new headquarters in Kildare Street, Dublin. The Chief Herald deals with an ever-increasing number of enquiries from abroad, especially from the USA and Australia, from people who are anxious to trace their roots and have sufficient documentary records of their families to enable them to do their research. There are also a number of professional research companies who will do this work for a specific fee.

Because a great many of Ireland's aristocratic families went abroad, their records and pedigrees are to be found mainly in the archives of France, Austria and Spain. These valuable historic documents are being explored and microfilmed for the National Library of Ireland, which should add considerably to research possibilities.

Brief Chronology
of Irish History

AD 200	Beginning of High Kingship at Tara, Meath
377-405	Niall of the Nine Hostages, High King
432	Saint Patrick comes as a Christian missionary
795	Vikings attack the Irish coast
852	Norse occupy Dublin and Waterford.
900-8	Cormac Mac Cullenan, King of Cashel
940-1014	Reign of High King, Brian Boru, killed at Battle of Clontarf
1119-56	Turlough Mór O Conor, High King
1134-71	Dermot MacMurrough, King of Leinster
1166-75	Rory O Conor, last native High King of Ireland
1170	Arrival of the Normans
1258	Gallowglasses (mercenary soldiers) come to Ulster from Scotland
1366	Statutes of Kilkenny enacted to prevent Anglo-Normans from integrating with Irish by using their language, laws or customs
1376-1417	Art MacMurrough, King of Leinster
1460	Irish parliamentary independence declared
1477-1513	Ireland ruled by Garret Mór Fitz-Gerald, Earl of Kildare
1513-34	Ireland ruled by Garret Óge Fitz-Gerald, Earl of Kildare
1536	Anglo-Irish parliament acknowledges Henry VIII of England as King of Ireland and head of the Church of Ireland. Suppression of the monasteries
1569-83	Revolt of the FitzGeralds, Earls of Desmond
1588	Spanish Armada wrecked off Irish coast
1592	Trinity College Dublin founded

1594	Beginning of Hugh O Neill, Earl of Tyrone's, nine-year war against the English
1598	Hugh O Neill, Earl of Tyrone, and Rory O Donnell, Earl of Tyrconnell, defeat the English at the Battle of the Yellow Ford
1602	Irish, reinforced by Spanish, defeated at Kinsale
1607	'Flight of the Earls' to Spain, led by O Neill and O Donnell
1608-10	British colony founded in Ulster
1641	Rising, which begins in Ulster, spreads
1649-50	Cromwellians devastate Ireland
1660	Restoration of Charles II
1689	Siege of Derry
1689	James II loses the English throne to his nephew and son-in-law, William of Orange
1690	Having rallied a Jacobite army in Ireland, James II, the deposed Stuart king, is defeated at the Battle of the Boyne by William of Orange
1691	11,000 'Wild Geese' soldiers sail for France
1692-1829	Exclusion of Catholics from parliament and all professions
1695	Penal Laws enforced
1778	Irish Volunteers organise
1782	Independent Dublin Parliament
1791	Society of United Irishmen founded
1798	Rising
1800	Act of Union. Ireland loses its independent parliament
1829	Catholic Emancipation inspired by Daniel O Connell
1842-8	Young Ireland movement
1845-7	The Great Famine. Population falls from eight millions to six-and-a-half millions
1867	Fenian Rising
1877-91	Charles Parnell
1916	Easter Rising
1918-21	Anglo-Irish war
1920	Six counties in Ulster vote themselves out

1922	Departure of British. Irish government takes over
1949	Repeal of External Relations Act. Ireland leaves Commonwealth and becomes a Republic
1955	Ireland joins the United Nations
1972	Ireland becomes a member of the European Economic Community

Ahearne *Ó hEachtighearna*

Hearne

Ahearne is practically the only Irish name spelled with the first letter of the alphabet. Originally it was Ó hEachtighearna, meaning 'lord of the horse'. The family was one of the very many descendants of the High King, Brian Boru. They were of the Dal gCáis (Dalcassians), an important sept in very early times in the counties of Clare and Limerick.

In time the name took many forms, of which Hearne is commonest today. Hearne is also to be found in England so that, lacking exact genealogical information, some Hearnes could be of English origin. Fleeing from religious persecution in the 17th and 18th centuries, many Ahernes found a new life in France, in the church, in the colleges and in the royal courts.

In 1754 a Limerick man, John Aheron, was author and illustrator of the first book on Irish architecture to be printed in Ireland. Another John who spelled his name Aherne was a United Irishman and a friend of Wolfe Tone. When he had to flee Ireland he became an officer in Napoleon's army.

In the 18th century, sometimes changing from Ahearne to Herne or Hearne, many emigrated to Canada, the USA and Australia.

Barry

Barrymore

The Barrys came from Wales with the Anglo-Norman invasion in 1170. They soon possessed a vast area of Co. Cork. There were so many Barrys that, to distinguish one from the other, they were known as Barry Mór (the Senior), Barry Óg (the Young), Barry Roe (the Red), Barry Maol (the Bald) and Barry Liadir (the Strong). They acquired titles such as Earl of Barrymore and Viscount of Buttevant. This Tipperary town got its name from the French 'boutez-en-avant' ('strike forward'), the rallying cry of the Barrys in their many battles.

Several Barrys were prominent in the arts and medicine. James Barry was a distinguished painter in London. The stage was strong in the Barry blood from 16th-century actor/dramatists to the trio of Barrymore stage and film actors of Philadelphia.

A Wexford man, John Barry, is revered as 'the father of the American Navy'.

Like so many of the nobility of the 18th and 19th centuries, the Barrys squandered their money, drinking and gambling until most of their splendid houses were gone.

A hunting lodge, Fota Island (outside Cork city) remains, taken over by Cork University. It is beautifully preserved and the furnishings include many Irish paintings.

During the Irish war of independence there were two Barry patriots, Kevin Barry and Commander Tom Barry.

Beirne *Ó Beirne*

Beirne, with or without the Ó, should never be confused with Byrne although they may sound alike. Beirne is thought to have originated from the Norse Bjorn.

The Beirnes settled around Co. Roscommon, where they formed an important sept. They do not appear in the records until about the 18th century, when two brothers from a family living in County Meath were sent to Rome to study for the priesthood. They returned home and went different ways. One became a parish priest while the other became a famous Archbishop of Meath of the Established Church. Beirnes are well recorded on the army rolls of France, Spain and America, where an Ó Beirne took a major part in the American Civil War. Their armorial bearings are particularly colourful. In the centre is an orange tree with a green lizard sitting at the base and, on one side, a red cross. A band of blue tops the shield with a silver crescent and a smiling sun.

Blake

Caddell

When they came with the Normans through Wales the Blake's name was Caddell. An especially dark-hued member of the family was nicknamed 'Le Blaca' (the Black). Thus the Blake name evolved. They settled in Galway city and county where, for hundreds of years, they were rich landowners and merchants and were numbered among the famous '14 Tribes of Galway'. Many of them were mayors and sheriffs of that city. They built castles all around Connacht, some of which survive. Apart from being statesmen they were also soldiers, going on the crusades and also taking part in Irish uprisings, including the decisive Battle of Kinsale.

An 18th-century Blake who inherited an enormous fortune got through it in a few years.

A Blake of Wicklow in the 19th century chartered a ship on which he sailed with his family and friends to Canada. There he was the progenitor of a succession of Toronto lawyers.

A branch of the Blake family settled in Co. Kildare where there are three Blakestowns.

In the west of Ireland there are Blake families of Gaelic origin whose name, Ó Blathmhaic, was anglicised to Blowick and then to Blake.

Boland *Ó Beolláin*

Bolan

The Bolands get their name from a Norwegian who came to Ireland very long ago. In Irish it is Ó Beolláin, while in English it used to be O Bolan. One branch of the family which claims descent from Mahon, one of King Brian Boru's brothers, went to Clare where they lived around Lough Derg. Ballybolan (the town of the Bolans) perpetuates their name. The other family settled in Sligo with their headquarters at Doonalton.

Little is recorded of the Bolands until the 20th century when they took part in the struggle for independence. A mission to America to collect funds and promote the Irish Republic internationally did very well. A Bolshevik party from Russia, who were doing far from well, asked for a loan of $20,000, offering what they said were some of the crown jewels as security. Harry Boland, who was with the delegation, gave the jewels to his mother for safe keeping. Harry was killed during the civil war. When Eamon de Valera came to power the Boland family gave him the jewels. It was not until 1948 that they were finally ransomed in London by the Russian Embassy there.

Frederick Boland was Irish Ambassador in London in the 1950s and also President of the United Nations. Eavan Boland, his daughter, is one of Ireland's leading poets. One of the oldest bakeries in Dublin, Boland's Mills, was the focus of much action during the Rising of 1916.

Boyle *Ó Baoighill*
O Boyle

There are two Boyle families, both of whom have made an impact on Ireland. In Irish Boyle is Ó Baoighill, which possibly means 'having profitable pledges'. They were a leading sept in Donegal, where their chieftain was duly inaugurated. The O Boyles of Boylagh owned much land in Co. Derry and had their castle at Desart in Co. Armagh.

Richard Boyle, who came as an 'adventurer' from England in the 16th century, has become known as 'the first colonial millionaire', the 1st Earl of Cork and the father of 15 children, most of whom — or their descendants — are among the Boyles featured in the *Dictionary of National Biography*. A scientific invention, Boyle's Law, was the work of one of his sons — the only untitled member of this opportunistic family. Richard Boyle 'acquired' the lands of most of the leading Irish families in Munster. When Sir Walter Raleigh was executed he bought his Waterford estate. At one time he made Lismore Castle there his principal seat.

In the 19th century Boyles from the north of Ireland began to go abroad; one to India and Japan to construct railroads; another to New York where he was a sculptor.

William Boyle was among the earliest dramatists to write for the infant Abbey Theatre in Dublin.

In recent years the Boyles have begun to resume their O prefix.

Browne

Brown   le Brun

The Irish Brownes have made their mark in history since they came with the Normans in the 12th century, when they were known as le Brun. They settled in Galway, married into the leading families and joined the '14 Tribes of Galway'.

A Browne from England was granted a huge area of Kerry by Elizabeth I. Ross Castle by the lakes of Killarney was Browne property. Lord Castlerosse, journalist and *bon viveur*, was the last of the Brownes to live in Kerry.

The Brownes spread through Ireland and went abroad in great numbers following the ill-fated Stuart monarchy. A soldier of fortune from Co. Limerick served in Russia where he rose to become Count George Browne at the court of Catherine the Great. A close relative was a Field Marshal in the Austrian army and a Count of the Empire.

William Brown from Co. Mayo was a founder of the Argentine navy. In America the Irish Browns were prominent in the army, science, the church, politics, education and commerce.

One of Ireland's rare cardinals was a Tipperary Browne.

Westport House in Co. Mayo, home of the Marquesses of Sligo of the Browne family, is in the stately home business and is managed by the heir, Lord Altamont. It is rich in the artefacts of Irish history and is visited by thousands every year.

Burke

Bourke   de Burgo

The Burkes descend from William the Conqueror and are the most numerous and most thoroughly integrated of all the Normans who came to Ireland in the 12th century. Originally their name was de Burgo (of the borough).

They were granted vast areas of O Conor land in Connacht. They multiplied fast and divided into a number of septs. The two senior were distinguished as MacWilliam Uachtar of Galway and MacWilliam Iochtar of Mayo.

Although a Burke is credited with building Galway city, they were not accepted into the '14 Tribes of Galway'. They were prominent in Anglo-Irish politics and exchanged their Gaelic chieftaincy of Clanricarde for the royal titles of Earl and Marquess of Clanricarde.

The most famous Burke is Edmund, a Dublin-born writer and orator who was a privy councillor in London at the time of the French Revolution.

During the exodus to Europe in the 17th century, there was a Regiment of Burke serving in France. They also went in great numbers to America and Australia.

Irish family pedigrees and the study of genealogy owe a great debt to the Tipperary family of Burke who founded *Burke's Peerage* and *Burke's Landed Gentry*. A descendant, Sir Bernard Burke, once held the office today styled Chief Herald of the Irish Genealogical Office.

Butler

The Butlers were one of the most outstanding of the Norman-Irish families. When Theobald Fitzwalter was created Chief Butler of Ireland by Herny II in 1177 the family came to be known as Butler. As they grew in importance they were created Earls of Ormond, the most important of many titles conferred on them. From their fortress at Gowran and, later, Kilkenny Castle, they feuded constantly with their neighbours and powerful rivals, the FitzGeralds, Earls of Kildare.

Anne Boleyn, one of the wives of Henry VIII and mother of Elizabeth I, was of Butler descent. The famous poet, William Butler Yeats, was also a kinsman.

The 7th Marquess and 31st Chief Butler lives in America. At the splendid Kilkenny Castle which the Butlers have handed over to the nation they gather from all over the world every three years for their family rally. A Butler archive has been set up in the castle tower. There are still Butlers in Europe, descendants of the 'Wild Geese'.

Butler is a very common name both in England and in Ireland. Lacking an authentic pedigree it would be impossible for anyone of the name to trace his ancestry to the Ormonds — or any other branch of this extensive family. Ulster is the only province the prolific Butlers failed to populate.

Cahill *MacCathail*

Cahill is one of the earliest recorded surnames. Originally a first name, Cathail is the Irish form of Charles which signifies 'valour'.

The first to bear this name was an important sept in south Galway in the very early times. Several distinct septs who developed independently spread to Munster, where there are no less than three Ballycahills in Co. Tipperary. There is also a Ballycahill in Co. Galway and another in Co. Clare — their original territory.

There are records of a 10th-century O Cahill martyr. The only other notable Cahill was a 19th-century crusading priest who collected in the USA for Catholic institutions in Ireland in the period of the Famine and Catholic Emancipation. In World War I three sons of the Ballyragget family in Co. Kildare were killed in action in France.

Cahill remains the most numerous name in Munster. The O prefix appears to have been dropped completely.

Carroll *Ó Cearbhaill*

MacCarvill

The O Carrolls trace their ancestry to a 3rd-century King of Munster, Oilioll Olum. Their name comes from Cearbhal (warlike champion), one of King Brian Boru's leading swordsmen at the Battle of Clontarf in 1014. Until the arrival of the Normans in 1170 there had been six different O Carroll septs headed by O Carroll Ely (Tipperary and Offaly) and O Carroll Oriel (Monaghan and Louth).

Much of their Tipperary territory was annexed by their powerful neighbours, the Norman Butlers. They were dispersed to various parts of the country, most particularly to Co. Offaly.

Father John Gleeson's *History of the Ely O Carroll Territory* was reprinted in 1982.

They were early churchmen who founded monasteries. They married into the royal blood of Ireland and England. They were incessant fighters, and fled with the 'Wild Geese' to Europe where they put their swords to use in the armies of France and other countries.

In the 20th century they founded Ireland's biggest tobacco industry, P. J. Carroll Ltd of Dundalk, Co. Louth.

An Ely O Carroll went to America at the end of the 17th century and was progenitor of a line of aristocratic and prominent American Carrolls who called their Maryland home Carrollton Manor.

O is their most numerous prefix but there is a separate MacCarroll sept which, in Ulster, has been anglicised to MacCarvill.

Clery *Ó Cleirigh*

Cleary   Clarke

Cleary is of some antiquity, dating from an early 9th-century Cléireach of the lineage of King Guaire of Connacht, renowned for his hospitality. His well-restored Dunguaire Castle on Galway Bay hosts medieval banquets in the summer.

Cléireach is the Irish work for 'clerk'. Early in the 16th century a family of O Clerys were instrumental in compiling a most valuable Irish manuscript, *The Annals of the Four Masters*. It was written mostly by a Franciscan monk in the ruined friary of Donegal.

The Clerys had been driven from Connacht to Ulster where they were poets, churchmen and *brehons* (lawgivers).

When the use of Gaelic names was forbidden the name was anglicised to Clarke. Lacking a family tradition or an official pedigree it is now impossible to distinguish between the Irish Clarkes who were O Clery and the many immigrant English Clarkes. Time has led to a happy integration and no one would question the Irishness of Thomas Clarke, one of the leaders of the 1916 Rising and first signatory to the Proclamation of the Irish Republic, Austin Clarke, the poet or Harry Clarke, the stained glass artist.

Two daughters of a Clery in Marseilles became Julie, Queen of Spain, and Desiree, Queen of Norway and Sweden, in Napoleonic times.

Collins   *Ó Coileáin*

There are very many of the name in England as well as in Ireland. Collins is an anglicisation of the Irish Ó Coileáin (whelp or young creature).

Until they were driven away by the Anglo-Norman invasion, the Ó Coileáin had been lords of the barony of Connello in Co. Limerick. They went further south to settle in West Cork, where the majority of the Collins are now to be found.

There were distinguished ecclesiastical Collins, including a patriot Jesuit who was hung in 1602, and a Dominican who led an attack on Bunratty Castle in 1647. An Ó Coileáin poet earned the epithet 'The Silver Tongue of Munster'.

An early emigrant, a Collins from Offaly, was a governor of Tasmania and a founder of Sydney. Another, who exchanged Wicklow for London, bred several generations of painters and authors, including Wilkie Collins who wrote *The Moonstone*.

There have been comparatively few Irish explorers, but a Collins has been recorded in the Arctic. In America a Collins line represented a family of shipowners who left Ireland in 1635.

The hero of the Collins family is Michael, 'The Big Fellow', whose promising political life was cut short in the civil war in 1922.

Connolly *Ó Conghaile*

Conghaile, the original Gaelic version of Connolly, means 'valorous'. They were an ancient sept of Connacht who in time separated and dispersed as three distinct families. They are still mainly based around counties Cork, Meath and Monaghan, where they were one of the 'Four Tribes of Tara'. In Monaghan, about 1591, Tirlogh O Connola is recorded as being chief of his name.

Because of his dazzling wealth the most famous Connolly was an early 18th-century William Connelly from Donegal whose family paved the way to success by conforming to the religion of the Establishment. A lawyer, he bought and sold the lands lost by the old Gaelic families exiled following the Battle of the Boyne. He was speaker in the Irish House of Commons. He began the building of the splendid Co. Kildare mansion, Castletown, now the headquarters of the very active Irish Georgian Society.

'Little Mo', the meteoric USA tennis star of the 50s, was a Connolly.

The patriot James Connolly, born in Scotland, was an Irish trade union pioneer and commanded the Republican army in Dublin. He signed the Proclamation of the Irish Republic just before his execution.

Cullen *Ó Cuillin*

Cullen in Irish is Ó Cuillin (holly tree). They were once a numerous clan in Wicklow until driven away by the O Byrnes and O Tooles. They moved to Co. Kildare, and there many have remained, giving their name to the town of Kilcullen.

They were in Wexford, too, recorded in the late 16th century as being gentry of Cullenstown.

This comparatively simple name has worked its way through an astonishing number of variations including Cullion, Culhoun, MacCullen and Cullinane. It could also be connected with a Scottish clan.

They were remarkable for their powerful clergymen, particularly bishops. There were a number of Cullen castles and mansions in the midlands, including ruined Liscarton Castle, once home of relatives of Ireland's first cardinal, Cardinal Paul Cullen.

In the early 19th century many sailed for the Argentine.

They were also prominent administrators in Australia. A shrub, *eucalyptus cullenii,* is named after a Cullen horticulturist there.

Curtin *Mac Cuirtin*

MacCurtin   Curtayne

O rather than the Mac is thought to be the correct Irish prefix to this name, although Mac is more likely to be found now. At one time the name in Irish was Cruitín (hunchback).

Originally the MacCruitíns' territory was on the Atlantic seaboard between Ennistymon and Corcomroe Abbey in Co. Clare. A MacCurtin who was chief of his sept was one of a long line of medieval scholars, poets and bards; a succession of them were hereditary bards to the aristocratic O Briens of nearby Thomond. Scattered by various internal battles, the Mac Curtins were dispersed around the country, especially to Limerick, Cork and, later, Dublin.

The MacCurtin family were prominent in France during the Revolution. One was a signatory to the National Convention, while a Major General Curtin was a leader of the Royalist opposition army.

A Cork man, Tomás MacCurtain, who commanded the Cork Brigade during the war of independence and was later Lord Mayor of Cork, was brutally murdered in 1920 by misguided militia.

Cusack *Cíomhsóg*

The Cusacks came from Guienne, a province of France, in 1211 in the wake of the Anglo-Norman invasion and were rewarded with a considerable acreage of Kildare and Meath. They integrated wholeheartedly with their Irish neighbours, and fought their way also to new possessions in Mayo, where they were known as MacIosóg.

They were on the side of James II at the Battle of the Boyne, and subsequently sailed with the many refugees to France to serve in the armies of Europe. One Cusack who had soldiered in Flanders turned to privateering on the high seas.

A distinguished and fashionable Dublin surgeon was the uncle of Margaret Cusack, 'the nun of Kenmare', a very emancipated and high-minded woman who dramatically changed her religious allegiance several times.

The Gaelic Athletic Association was founded in 1884 largely through the inspiration of Michael Cusack from Clare.

Cyril Cusack is a much acclaimed actor of stage and screen who is ably followed by his daughters.

Daly *Ó Dálaigh*

In Irish the name is Ó Dálaigh, which was the word for a meeting place, as in Dail Eireann.

The Ó Dálaigh ancestry goes back to the 4th century, to Niall of the Nine Hostages, the High King who had his palace at Tara, Co. Meath, and from whom descend also the O Neills and the O Donnells.

They are very prominent in records dating from the 12th to the 18th century, when their extraordinary genius for bardic literature was manifest in the bardic school set up by Cuconnacht Ó Dálaigh in Westmeath.

From the 11th to the 17th century they were hereditary poets and minstrels to most of the leading families.

Their outstanding churchman was a Dominican friar, Daniel, who, fleeing religious persecution, went to Europe where he founded colleges in Louvain and Lisbon.

From a Daly family, Barons of Dunsanele and Clan Conal in Co. Galway, came six mayors of the city of Galway. This family emigrated to the colonies, America and Australia, where they distinguished themselves as administrators and, in Britain, in the army.

In the 1970s Chief Justice Cearbhaill Ó Dálaigh of County Wicklow was with the Court of Justice of the European Economic Community and, afterwards, for a brief period, President of the Republic of Ireland.

Dillon

The Dillons are a widespread and well-recorded family who in the 800 years since their arrival from Brittany as de Leon have merged indistinguishably with the Irish. They were granted great acreages where they prospered and grew so numerous that their lands around Longford, Westmeath and Kilkenny were called Dillon's Country.

Offshoots of the family went to Mayo and Sligo, where the head of that family was Viscount Dillon of Costello-Gallen. The Dillons acquired many peerages and played an active role in the tangle of 17th-century Anglo-Irish politics. They built many castles but lost them and their land because of their adherance to Catholicism.

Following the devastation perpetrated by the Cromwellians they fled to France, where they raised a Regiment of Dillon in which Irish refugees distinguished themselves. During the French Revolution Theobald, Count Dillon, a Field Marshal of France who had fought in the American War of Independence, was its colonel.

Portlick Castle, Glasson, Co. Meath, is one of the best preserved of their remaining castles. Clonbrock House in Ballinasloe, Galway, where the Dillons had lived since 1575, was sold a few years ago and its invaluable archives were presented by Luke Dillon-Mahon to the nation.

Doherty *Ó Dochartaigh*

There are many variants of O Doherty of which Doherty is the most usual. In Irish it is Ó Dochartaigh, which is supposed to mean 'obstructive'. They are descended from the powerful 4th-century King Niall of the Nine Hostages. Their earliest headquarters was the Inishowen Peninsula in Donegal.

Their promising but foolish chief, Cahir Ó Doherty, in an ill-conceived rebellion attacked Derry and was massacred. This uprising let to the Plantation of Scottish settlers in the six counties of Ulster, laying the base for continuing strife.

Cahir's brother joined the 'Wild Geese' in their flight to Europe. His accredited descendant is in Cadiz, Spain and styles himself 'The O Doherty'.

From colonial resistance in Ireland the O Dohertys fled to Scotland and England where they merged successfully. Later they emigrated to Australia and north America.

The O Dohertys are still plentiful in Donegal where, since 1981, they have been planning a clan rally for 1985. Already there has been a clan rally in the USA, where there is an O Doherty Family Research Association.

Donoghue *Ó Donnchadha*
Dunphy

There are a variety of ways in which this important and numerous Irish patronymic can be spelled. In Irish it is Ó Donnchadha, coming from the personal name Donnchadh (Donogh).

At first there were O Donoghue septs in Cork and Kerry, where Ross Castle was their fortress on Lough Lene, Killarney. Other septs moved up to Galway, Kilkenny and Cavan, where their descendants are usually Donohue. They claim descent from a King of Munster who fought at Clontarf in 1014.

In Kerry their chieftain was O Donoghue Mór of Ross Castle, while the other was O Donoghue of the Glens, also in Kerry. His descendant is styled 'The O Donoghue', one of approximately fifteen chieftains who have been officially recognised as such.

A 12th-century O Donoghue founded the beautiful Jerpoint Abbey in Co. Kilkenny. A namesake of the present O Donoghue, Geoffrey O Donoghue of the Glens, was a revered 17th-century poet and scholar at Glenflesk, Killarney.

In Kilkenny some of the O Donoghue sept changed their name to the more high-sounding Dunphy. In the 18th century the O Donoghues were with the Irish diaspora who served in the continental armies. Ironically, the last Spaniard to rule Mexico bore the name Juan O Donju.

Doyle *Ó Dubhghaill*

When the Norsemen came to Ireland about the 9th century they were called dubh-ghall (dark foreigner). In Irish Doyle is Dubhghall and it is assumed that they were Norsemen, which seems to be borne out by the fact that this very numerous name is so prevalent on the south-east coast, particularly around Wexford.

They are not mentioned in the ancient Irish genealogies. However, from the 17th century on they feature, particularly in the armies of Europe and, later, Britain, where at one time there were six Doyles from Kilkenny all with the rank of major general.

There were many distinguished Doyle ecclesiastics. Arthur Conan Doyle, the inventor of the great detective Sherlock Holmes, was the descendant of a famous family of artists and writers who had originated from Dublin.

In comparatively recent times Jack Doyle, 'the Gorgeous Gael', blazed a starry trail across the boxing rings, the footlights and the divorce courts.

Duffy *Ó Dubthaigh*

The Irish Ó Dubhthaig gives a clue to this name. Dubh means 'black'. Little is recorded of their origins except that in the 7th century they were prominent in the church in Monaghan. At that time, too, the patron saint of Raphoe in Donegal was Dubhtach. In Ulster the name has been transformed to Dowey.

Exceptionally gifted craftsmen, in the 12th century they enriched monasteries and churches working for the High King, Turlough O Conor.

In Roscommon there was such a multitude of Duffys there is a town there called Lissyduffy.

In the 19th century Sir Charles Gavan Duffy was the progenitor of a succession of able lawyers. He went to Australia where he was Premier of Victoria and left many distinguished descendants. His daughter founded Dublin's famous Irish language school.

An ex-Irish army officer and garda, General Eoin O Duffy, organised an Irish brigade to fight for Franco during the Spanish Civil War.

In the 19th century James Duffy founded a Dublin publishing firm which is still in existence. Duffy's is one of the oldest circuses still touring the Irish roads.

Dunne   *Ó Duinn*

Dunn

Although there are Dunnes in England, it is a very numerous Irish name and means 'brown'. The sept predominated in the midlands, in Leix, where at one time they were Lords of Iregan, one of the important families in Leinster.

In the 12th century the chief poet of Leinster was Giolla-na-Naomh O Dunn.

They were very active in the Jacobite wars, and afterwards they emigrated to the USA, where they served in the church, the law and the army.

In Ulster the more usual form of the name is Dunn.

A five times President of the Royal College of Physicians in Ireland came from Scotland in the 17th century. Sir Patrick Dun's Hospital in Dublin is his lasting memorial.

In recent years Dunne's Stores, a countrywide chain store group, has become a household word.

Egan   *Mac Aodhagáin*
Keegan

MacAodhagáin means 'son of Aodh' (anglicised to Hugh). Seldom using their Mac prefix, in modern times the name has become Egan. Their origins are in Galway, Roscommon and Leitrim. They were scattered to Tipperary, Kilkenny and Offaly.

For generations they had held the hereditary office of *ollav* or lawyer to the ruling families. Following the destruction of the old Gaelic order they held high office in the church, while also taking part in many battles.

Two Pierce Egans, father and son, were popular writers in 19th-century London. Another London-born Egan who styled himself 'The MacEgan', though not officially accredited, was a painter of distinction.

In the USA there were many Egans, one of whom became known as 'the Dean of the Diplomatic Corps'.

When Irish names had to be changed to their nearest English equivalent Egan sometimes became Keegan, especially in Dublin and Wicklow.

Thanks to a family of lawyers in Castlebar, Redwood Castle in Lorrha, Tipperary, has been beautifully restored and is the setting for Clan MacEgan rallies.

FitzGerald

Fitz means 'son' and since Maurice, son of Gerald, came with the Norman invaders in 1170 the FitzGeralds proliferated and became one of the most powerful families. Their leaders were the Fitzgeralds, Earls of Kildare and Dukes of Leinster, and the Fitzgeralds who were Earls of Desmond (Kerry and Cork).

In the 16th century Garret Mór, 8th Earl of Kildare, was for 40 years regarded in all but name as King of Ireland. The Earls of Desmond were in rebellion for many terrible years and became extinct when the 16th Earl was killed in Elizabethan times.

They built splendid castles, a number of which are still in good condition. In succeeding generations many FitzGeralds who opposed English rule were imprisoned or executed in the Tower of London.

An early Earl of Desmond created his three illegitimate sons Knight of Glin, Knight of Kerry and the (no longer surviving) White Knight.

The FitzGeralds have seldom been out of politics. A modern Garret FitzGerald has been three times Taoiseach (Prime Minister).

Gallagher   *Ó Gallchobhair*

The Gallaghers, who were one of the principal septs of Donegal, are still very numerous there. They claimed absolute seniority over the Cineal Connail, the royal family of Connall Gulban, son of the great 4th-century King Niall of the Nine Hostages.

A translation from the Irish for their name, gallchobhair (foreign help), was possibly acquired in the three centuries when they were marshalls in the armies of the O Donnells.

Their notabilities in the main were clerical. Six O Gallaghers were Bishop of Raphoe in Donegal.

Redmond O Gallagher, Bishop of Derry, helped the Armada sailors wrecked off Donegal and was executed by the English.

Frank Gallagher, a journalist who fought in the civil war, was the first editor of De Valera's newspaper, the *Irish Press*. Patrick Gallagher of Donegal, known as 'Paddy the Cope', initiated the idea of co-operative farming.

Guinness *MagAonghusa*

Magennis

In 1894 sixteen different versions were recorded of the ancient Ulster surname, MagAonghusa. It means 'son of Aonghus' (one choice). Their ancestry goes back to a 5th-century chief of Dal Araidhe. By the 12th century they had become lords of Iveagh in County Down, where they had their fortress at Rathfriland.

Although they played along with the Elizabethans, they were with Hugh O Neill at the victorious Battle of the Yellow Ford in 1598.

They survived disastrous defeat at Kinsale and had their 22,000 acres restored. Magennis of Iveagh was created Viscount. They had several distinguished bishops in the family, both Catholic and Protestant. A Viscount Iveagh sat in the 'Patriot Parliament' in 1689, the last such until 1922. Shortly after the Battle of the Boyne the Magennis's joined the exodus to serve in the armies of Austria, France, Spain and later, America.

The Guinness name has been stamped on the Irish consciousness since 1759, when Arthur Guinness set up his enormously successful brewery by the River Liffey in Dublin. The Guinness family endeared themselves by their generous contributions in charitable institutions. The company, affectionately known as 'Uncle Arthur', was one of the corner stones of the Irish economy.

Healy *Ó hÉildhe*

Hely

The modern Healy/Hely is an amalgam of two distinct septs, Ó hÉildhe (éildhe means 'claimant') whose chieftains were centred on Lough Arrow in Co. Sligo, and Ó hÉilaighthe (éaladhach means 'ingenious') who settled in Donoughmore in Co. Cork.

They were all dispossessed of their lands by the Cromwellians. Even before that crucial period Healys had gone abroad for their education, especially for the priesthood.

When John Hely of Cork married a Hutchinson heiress he added her name to his and began a line of distinguished Hely Hutchinsons who were Earls of Donoughmore. The first John Hely Hutchinson was Provost of Trinity College Dublin. In 1974 the elderly Earl and Countess of Donoughmore were abducted for a while from their ancestral home, Knocklofty, in County Tipperary. They have since sold Knocklofty.

In the 18th and 19th centuries there were a number of prominent painters in the Healy family, including a stained glass artist. Tim Healy of Bantry was a journalist, wit and politician in London. He was the first Governor General of the Irish Free State from 1922 to 1928. Ulster born Cahir Healy has been described as 'one of the sanest and most farseeing leaders of the northern nationalists'.

Hennessy *Ó hAonghusa*

Hensey Henchy

Ó hAonghusa comes from a personal name, Aonghus or Angus. There are as many places called Ballyhennessy in Connacht and Munster as there were branches of this family who have totally discarded the O prefix, gradually transforming their name to Hennessy, Hensey and Henchy.

The leading sept were in Offaly, near Kilbeggan. Another sept had their lands on the borders between Meath and Dublin. With the arrival of the Normans in 1170 they fled to Limerick, Tipperary and Cork where the majority of the name is still to be found.

One of their strongholds, Ballymacmoy near Mallow, Co. Cork, has only recently been abandoned by the Hennessys.

They served with great distinction in the French army and at the court, where they were given titles of nobility. It was an Irish member of this martial family, retired from the French army, who discovered the formula for the brandy of Cognac which continues to keep their name before the public. They also had an eye for horses and one of their French thoroughbreds won the Triple Crown in the Hennessy Gold Cup.

A member of the distinguished Pope Hennessy family of Cork, an MP for Westmeath, was the first Catholic Conservative member to hold an Irish seat.

Higgins *Ó hUigín*

Although there are also Higgins of British origin, in Ireland the name is an ancient one, a translation from the Irish Ó hUigín (uigín meaning 'knowledge'). Earlier, they were a branch of the Westmeath O Neills. Many of them moved away to Co. Sligo where, until recently, they owned much land.

From the 13th to the 17th century there were eight Ó hUigín poets, including one who was also a bishop. Following the submergence of the poets and bards the O Higgins changed to medicine and the sciences, where they excelled.

One of the Meath family was an 18th-century Viceroy of Peru. His son, the famous Bernardo O Higgins, Liberator of Chile, was its first President. Their name is commemorated in Chile in the province called O Higgins.

Two Higgins qualify for the list of Irish eccentrics. One, a divinity graduate of Dublin, preached sedition in London, where he also kept a house of ill fame. The other, 'The Sham Squire', followed every means of accumulating money; changing his religion, marrying an heiress, gambling, journalism, informing.

Many Higgins sailed for Australia. A son of a Co. Down family was Attorney General there.

The founder of the Civic Guards, patriot and lawyer Kevin O Higgins, was assassinated in 1927.

Hogan   *Ó hOgáin*

Óg is Irish for 'young'. An Ó hOgáin sept descends from the celebrated 10th-century King of Ireland, Brian Boru. They were of the Dalcassian people who inhabited Thomond, around Clare and Limerick. They divided to spread across Tipperary, where their chieftain has his fortress at Nenagh.

The Hogans lost their lands under the Cromwellians but had some re-granted by Charles II.

In 1691 'Galloping Hogan' became the hero of Sarsfield's destruction of the Williamite siege train at Ballyneety.

Later some went to Europe. There was a Hogan surgeon in the Irish brigade in France, and they were with T. J. Meagher in the Irish-American brigades in the Civil War of the 1860s.

John Hogan from Waterford reached great eminence as a sculptor in Rome, only driven home by the revolution of 1848 to enrich Ireland with his beautiful statues.

In the 19th century the Hogans contributed to literature. Edmund, a Jesuit priest, edited books on Irish place names and biographies. Michael, 'the Bard of Thomond', wrote popular verse. Austin Hogan of Clare founded the Transport Workers Union of America, while another man from Clare, Patrick Hogan, patriot, trade unionist and writer, was a senator and speaker in Dáil Éireann.

Joyce

The Joyce name has been deeply embedded in Connacht since they arrived there by sea in the wake of the Norman invaders. Joyce comes from the French personal name Joy. They quickly intermarried with strong local families like the O Briens, Princes of Thomond.

A huge clan, they owned vast territory in the barony of Ross (Co. Galway), known today as Joyce's Country, and were admitted into the elite of the '14 Tribes of Galway'. There were Joyce bishops and crusaders to the Holy Land. One who was captured en route was shown buried treasure by an eagle. When he escaped with this wealth he used it to build the walls of Galway city.

A Joyce captured in the Middle East learned the art of gold and silver smithing. It is he who is credited with the origins of the Claddagh ring.

A family literary strain is epitomised in James Joyce, playwright, poet, musician and author of *Ulysses*.

During World War II the infamous William Joyce broadcast Nazi propaganda from Germany. Of mixed Irish-English-American background, his English affiliations caused him to be hanged for treason when he was captured after the war.

Kavanagh   *Caomhánach*

Cavanagh

The Kavanaghs are direct descendants of Diarmuid MacMurrough, 12th-century King of Leinster, who initiated the Anglo-Norman invasion. He sent his son Donal to be educated at Wexford with the monks at Kilcavan (Cill Caomhan, i.e. St Kevin's Church). Perhaps to distinguish him from the other Donals the King's son was called Caomhanach, anglicised to Kavanagh.

Donal, alias Kevin/Kavanagh, was not chosen to succeed as king. He was compensated with large areas of Wexford and Carlow, still the base of the numerous Kavanaghs.

Art MacMurrough, the first to style himself Kavanagh, was King of Leinster for 42 years. He fought hard to oust the invaders. His struggle was continued by a succession of McMurrough Kavanagh kings until the time of Henry VIII.

Art McMurrough Kavanagh, a direct descendant of Leinster kings and a 13th child, was born lacking legs or arms. Thanks to the devotion of his mother he grew to be an athlete, sportsman and scholar. He became heir to the great Borris estate, married, fathered seven children, and was an MP. He has inspired many books.

A man from a Monaghan farm, Patrick Kavanagh, is one of the leading 20th-century Irish poets.

Castles at Enniscorthy and Ferns, Borris House and the Kavanagh drinking horn in Trinity College Dublin are tangible reminders of these kings of Leinster.

Keane *Ó Cathain*

Kane

The Keane/Kane family were originally Mac Cathain of West Clare, Ó Cahain of Ulster and Ó Céin of Munster. In time their anglicisation as Keane, or Kane, made their topographical origins difficult to define. Their name derives from the personal name Cian.

Blosky O Kane, who slew the heir to the throne in the 12th century, was the forefather of the MacCloskeys. Aibhne Ó Catháin's descendants became the McEvinneys.

The Kanes tend to be numerous in Ulster while the Keanes are usually to be found in Munster and Connacht.

For centuries, both at home and far afield, the Kanes/Keanes were active military men. In the 18th century there were 14 O Keane brothers serving in Europe.

In the 19th century, Kanes and Keanes were prominent in the sciences, architecture and the arts. The great acting family of Edmund Kean and his son Charles had their origins in Waterford. The popular playwright-publican, John B. Keane, is a Kerryman.

John Keane and James Keane, at different periods, were two of many Irish-Americans who filled the post of Bishop of Dubuque in Iowa, USA.

Keogh *MacEochaidh*
Kehoe Hoey Hoy

MacEochaidh—it needs an Irish speaker to pronounce it—was anglicised to Keogh, pronounced Kee-oh. Eochaidh, a personal name, was adopted by a family which comprised three distinct septs. Their territory was Limerick and Ballymackeogh; the second sept were lords of Moyfinn around Athlone and Roscommon (known as Keogh's Country); the third sept, the MacKeoghs of Leinster, is the most recorded. They were related to the O Byrnes, for whom they were hereditary bards. In 1534 Maolmuire MacKeogh was the finest poet in Leinster, one of a line of poets of the name.

Following the Norman invasion they moved south to Wexford, where they are now more usually known as Kehoe.

John Keogh of Dublin was an early pioneer of Catholic Emancipation. William Keogh of Keoghville, Galway, a wealthy judge, fell foul of the Fenians and the Home Rulers, who hounded him out of Ireland.

Myles Keogh of Carlow has become an American folk hero for his part in the disastrous incident at the Little Big Horn.

In some cases Keogh was anglicised to O Hoey or Hoy. They were of the sept which was descended from the early kings of Ulster.

Another offshoot who were Limerick landowners spelled their name K'Eogh. They also had property in Holland and Switzerland.

Kirwan *Ó Ciardubháin*

The origins of the Kirwans go back to Heremon of the Milesians who probably came from Spain. In Irish their name is Ciardubháin ('black'). Louth was one of their earlier settlements. When they moved to Galway, with the Darcys, they were the only native families accepted into the '14 Tribes of Galway'.

They have a long history of eminent ecclesiastics, both Catholic and Protestant. As priests and soldiers they had close connections with Europe. Richard Kirwan of Cregg Castle, Galway, who was 6ft 4in. tall, was with Dillon's Regiment at Fontenoy. His fondness for duelling caused his dismissal from the French army, whereupon he changed to the Austrian army. In the 18th century there were a number of Kirwan medical men in France. James Kirwan was a physician to the indolent Louis XV.

From Château Kirwan in the Medoc comes the prestigious French wine which still bears their name.

A Dublin Kirwan precipitated the 1803 revolution and was executed with Robert Emmet.

Richard Kirwan of the Cregg Castle family was an amazingly versatile man, a true eccentric. He left the Jesuits and, in time, became a most learned member of the Royal Dublin Society and was first President of the Royal Irish Academy.

Lacy *de Léis*

de Lacy

The de Lacys took their name from Lascy in Normandy, from which they came to conquer England and then Ireland.

The founder of this once great Norman family was Hugh de Lacy, who was given 800,000 acres in Meath, deposing the royal O Melaghlins (now known as MacLaughlin). Hugh married Rose, daughter of O Conor, King of Connacht, and built castles, including Trim Castle by the River Boyne.

His son, Walter, acquired land in Co. Down and was created Earl of Ulster by the English. Realising the de Lacys were growing too powerful, King John expelled them to Scotland for a while. In the 16th century the de Lacys joined with the native Irish in the struggle to expel the Elizabethan usurpers.

A strongly military family, when they had to leave Ireland with the 'Wild Geese' they joined the Irish brigades in France. Peter Lacy of Limerick, following the Battle of the Boyne, went to Poland and Russia, where Peter the Great employed him to train the élite of his army. As Peter, Count Lacy, after 50 years in Russia, he retired to his estates there. His son, Count Franz Moritz, born in St Petersburgh, served the Empress of Austria as Field Marshal. There are still Lacys in Russia.

Although the de Lacys have long since left their ancestral estates at Ballingarry, Bruff and Bruree they are still numerous in all four provinces.

Lynch   *Ó Loingsigh*

Lynch, one of the most numerous and distinguished Irish surnames, is a fusion of two different races. One forebear was de Lynch who came with the Normans. The other was Labradh Longseach (mariner), who in the 6th century BC was King of Ireland. These Lynches settled in Clare, Sligo and Limerick, with a branch in Donegal.

The Norman Lynches were leaders of the '14 Tribes of Galway'. From 1484–1654 Galway city had 84 Lynch mayors. To protect their families and their wealth they built strong castles in Connemara and in Galway city.

Dominic Lynch founded a school there, attended by thousands of scholars. His son was Archdeacon of Tuam and an historian. He had to flee to France and Spain with many other learned Irish priests.

The Blosse Lynch family of Co. Mayo (the Blosse came from a marriage) were 19th-century travellers and merchants who explored the Euphrates, the Tigris in Persia and sailed into Baghdad.

The Lynches went to Australia, the Argentine and Chile, where Patrick Lynch is remembered as 'the foremost Chilean naval hero'. Elizabeth Lynch and the Paraguayan dictator, Francisco Lopez II, held sway there for a dozen years.

Thomas Lynch, a plantation owner, signed the American Declaration of Independence.

Jack Lynch of Cork, who won six All-Ireland medals for hurling and Gaelic football, was Taoiseach for two terms in the 1970s.

MacCabe   *Mac Cába*

In the middle ages Irish chieftains imported fighting men from Scotland to augment their forces. Many of these mercenaries, known as gallowglasses, were the MacCabes who came from Inis Gall (the Isles of the Norsemen) in the Hebrides. They served the O Reillys and the O Rourkes of Leitrim and Cavan. It is thought their name comes from the peculiar hats they wore; caba means 'hat' or 'cap'.

They remained in Ireland to found their own sept. One of these, Cathaoir MacCabe, was a close friend of Turlough O Carolan, the greatest of the MacCabe bards. O Carolan offended MacCabe by writing a premature lament on his death. When O Carolan died Cathaoir wrote a beautiful lament for him.

A Belfast MacCabe prevented the shipowners there from using their vessels for the slave trade. His son, William Putnam MacCable, who was very active during the 1798 rising, eluded all his pursuers because of his uncanny talent for disguise. He escaped to Normandy where he followed his father's business by setting up a cotton mill.

They can boast a cardinal; Edward Cardinal MacCabe (1816-1885).

Eugene MacCabe, a Monaghan farmer, wrote a number of popular plays which were performed at Dublin's Abbey Theatre.

MacCarthy *MacCarthaigh*

MacCarthy is one of the most ancient and numerous surnames in Ireland, going back to a 3rd-century King of Munster. The surname derives from Carthac, a 12th-century descendant.

A MacCarthy king and bishop, Cormac, built the much admired chapel on the holy Rock of Cashel, still known as Cormac's chapel. The MacCarthys were good builders, and the remains of their fine castles are to be found all over Munster.

Blarney is the most famous, and there lived Cormac MacCarthy, whose evasive answers to Queen Elizabeth's letters demanding his submission roused her to call his protestations 'blarney'. So started the legend that kissing the Blarney Stone would convey eloquence. There was no lack of eloquence in the MacCarthy family, from whom has come a succession of poets and writers.

Florence MacCarthy, Lord of Carberry, dared to strengthen his territories by marrying his cousin, Lady Ellen of the Clan Carthy, which also displeased the English monarch. Florence was eventually incarcarated in the Tower of London, where he spent 37 years occupied with writing a history of Ireland, published 200 years after his death.

In Ireland the Muckross estate, by the Lakes of Killarney — once the home of the MacCarthy Mór — is looked after now by the state and is open to the public.

MacDermot   *MacDiarmada*
MacDermott   Kermode

The brother of Muiredach Mullethan, King of Connacht in the 8th century, Maelruanaidh Mór (Mulrooney) was Prince of Moylurg in Roscommon. It was from a 12th-century descendant, Dermot, King of Moylurg, that they adopted the surname Dermot (free man).

Their territories in Roscommon and Sligo were known as 'MacDermot's Country'. They built their fortress on the legendary island of Lough Cé. A 16th-century chieftain, Brian MacDermot, instigated the writing of the *Annals of Lough Cé*, now in Trinity College Dublin.

In ancient times there were three MacDermot septs; those who descended from Muiredach Mullethan, forebears of the kingly O Conors of Connacht; the MacDermottroes whose seat was at Alderford, Roscommon; the MacDermotts who were chiefs of Airtech. Following the ill-fated Stuarts they lost much of their property and their chief seat moved to Coolavin in Sligo. The only Irish family to have a princely title, they are also chiefs of their name. Although their kinsmen went abroad, the Princes of Coolavin remained in Ireland where, in the 19th century, they reached high office. The present Prince of Coolavin, 'The MacDermot', Sir Dermot MacDermot, a former ambassador in the British Diplomatic Service, has compiled their history for his family.

There are variations in the spelling of MacDermot, but the most unusual and rare is Kermode.

MacGrath *MacRaith*

Magraith Magraw

There are several variations in the modern spelling of this numerous name, which originally was MacRaith. Raith, a first name, means 'prosperity'. There were two septs. In Donegal and Fermanagh the Macgraths were hereditary guardians of Saint Daveog's monastery at Lough Derg. They lived in Termon Castle, near Pettigo. The other sept were from Clare and Limerick, where the MacGraths were poets and their patrons were the kingly O Briens of Thomond. They were also presidents of the famous school for bards at Cahir, Tipperary.

The notorious, avaricious Myler Magrath came from the Donegal sept. Originally a Franciscan friar, he trimmed his beliefs to whatever religion suited his ambition. He was Anglican Bishop of Cashel during Elizabeth's reign. At one time he held four bishoprics, both Catholic and Anglican. He married twice and lived to be 100 years old. His son, Edmund, acted as a spy for the Cromwellians who confiscated much of the McGrath possessions and burned their castle outside Waterford.

As exiles in France both the McGraths and the Magraths are well recorded. A Magrath emigré, a veteran of the American Civil War, was governor of California, while a McGraw was governor of Washington DC.

One of those who helped to build up the Irish economy was Joseph McGrath, a veteran of the Rising and a government minister. He was one of the founders of the Irish Hospitals Sweepstakes and he helped to revive the old Waterford crystal industry.

Maguire   *MagUidhir*

MacGuire   McGuire

The Macguire name is first recorded in 956, but it was not until the 14th century that they became the most prominent of the Fermanagh septs. The name comes from the Irish, MagUidhir (Mag meaning 'Mac'), and means 'pale coloured'. They were kinsmen of the kingly O Neills and the princely O Connells of Ulster. From the 15th century a succession of learned Maguire bishops is recorded.

The Maguire stronghold was on Lough Erne, where they were Barons of Enniskillen. Their greatest chieftain, Hugh Maguire, led the Irish army which defeated the English at the Battle of the Yellow Ford. A descendant, Conor, notorious for his bungling of the Ulster nobles' plot to capture Dublin castle, was subsequently executed in the Tower of London.

Many of the Maguires followed the exodus to Europe where their aristocratic lineage was recognised by the French court.

Thomas Maguire (d. 1889) was the first Roman Catholic to be made a Fellow of Trinity College, where he was Professor of Moral Philosophy.

There were many distinguished Maguires in the USA. Those who spell the name MacGuire, or McGuire, usually originated in Connacht. One of these was chief surgeon to Stonewall Jackson, and Professor at Virginia Medical College.

Enniskillen Castle, their Fermanagh stronghold, is in good repair and there are several remains of their seats in that area.

MacKenna *Mac Cionaoith*

In Irish the name is MacCionaoda, meaning 'son of Cionaoid'. Who this was is not known, for little is recorded of the MacKennas until comparatively recently. An Ulster family, they were lords of Truagh, the present Trough in County Monaghan.

The most outstanding characteristic of the MacKennas is their literary talent. Theobald MacKenna, a political moderate at the time of Wolfe Tone, wrote tirelessly promoting parliamentary reform and Catholic Emancipation. In the late 19th century there were three Stephen MacKenna writers, two novelists and one journalist who had fought for the Greeks and translated Plautinus. Lambert MacKenna, a Jesuit priest, edited many books in the Irish language on bardic poetry and history.

The most colourful of the MacKennas was John (later Juan) from Tyrone who studied engineering in Spain and went to South America where the viceroy, Ambrosio O Higgins, made good use of his skills in the defence of Peru. John MacKenna died later following a dramatic duel in Buenos Aires.

The talented MacKennas are also well known for acting. Siobhan McKenna is the doyenne of Irish actresses, and T. P. McKenna is a popular stage, screen and TV actor.

Martin McKenna left Kilkenny for Australia to become a successful brewer, farmer and founder of a big family in Kyneton, Victoria.

MacMahon *Mac Mathghamhna*

Mohan   Vaughan

MacMahon (in modern Irish MacMahuna, meaning 'son of a bear') represents two distinct septs. One descends from the royal O Briens and was of Corcabaskin, Clare, while the other sept were known as Lords of Oriel in Louth and Monaghan. The two chieftaincies became extinct in the 18th century with the deaths of Teige of Corcabaskin at Kinsale and Hugh Óge of Oriel who was hung at Tyburn.

Hugh Óge's cousin, Heber MacMahon, was a European-educated bishop, a member of the Catholic Confederation and a poet. He was also an army general—for which he had to suffer martyrdom.

Folklore credits Máire Rua (Red) MacMahon with diverse amorous attachments. In the records she had one husband who died young. Then she chose to marry Conor O Brien and together they built the handsome castle of Lemaneagh in Clare. When he was killed, to protect her large family and property she ruthessly married a Cromwellian. She managed to elude a charge of murder.

The outstanding MacMahon is Edmonde Patrice, a descendant of an ennobled family of France who had fled there with the 'Wild Geese'. A brilliant professional soldier, this field marshal was for six years President of France.

Of the numerous MacMahons who emigrated to Australia one was Prime Minister from 1971-2.

When Mac is dropped from MacMahon it indicates an entirely different name, one which can also be Mohan and which, at some time, was also transformed to Vaughan.

MacNamara
MacConmara

MacNamara means 'son of the hound of the sea'. Their territory was the far west coast of Clare and their ancestor, Cas, was the first chieftain of the powerful Dalcassians. The MacMahons had the right to inaugurate the O Brien chieftains or kings.

The MacNamaras became compulsive builders — 57 castles, fortresses and abbeys are credited to them in Clare, including Quin Abbey and the famous castles of Bunratty and Knappogue.

There were two septs. The MacNamara Fion (fair) held the chiefdom of Clancullen West, while MacNamara Reagh (swarthy) was chief of the East. Their titles and possessions were wrested from them by the marauding Cromwellians, which drove them to seek outlets in Europe and the new world.

They were natural seamen. Count MacNamara, a commodore of the French fleet and diplomat in the Far East, was assassinated there in the backlash from the French Revolution because of his royalist connections.

Donnchadha Ruadh MacConmara was educated for the priesthood in Rome, but was expelled. He turned to teaching and poetry, for which he has become best known. He travelled much and had many wild adventures, changed his religion to suit his prospects and lived to be 95.

One of the MacNamara houses, at Ennistymon, is now the Falls Hotel. Here was born Caitlin, wife of Dylan Thomas, and her father, Francis, poet and eccentric.

Malone   *Ó Maoileoin*

The Malone name comes from Maoileoin, which meant 'one who served St John'. Early Malone history is centred on Offaly, where they had their estate at Ballynahown. They were kinsmen of the O Conors, who were kings in nearby Connacht.

Clonmacnoise, the great ecclesiastical seat of learning, was in their territory and a number of Malones presided there as abbots or bishops. The Malones who supported James II had to flee to Europe, where they can be traced in the armies and in the records of France and Spain. In Italy William Malone was a President of the Irish College in Rome.

The Malones of Baronstown changed to the Anglican faith, which saved them from losing their lands in Westmeath.

Of two Sylvester Malones, both priests, one was a church historian and Irish language enthusiast, while the second went to Brooklyn where he worked for the relief of the victims arriving on famine ships.

Walter Malone, who also went to the USA, wrote the epic poem on the Mississippi river where the American Indians were cruelly treated by the Spaniards.

'Molly Malone' is one of Dublin's outstanding characters, and every Dubliner can sing the popular ditty describing how she 'Wheeled her wheelbarrow through streets broad and narrow, Singing cockles and mussels, alive, alive oh!'

Martin *Ó Martain*
Martyn Gilmartin

The Irish Martins were kinsmen of the O Neills of Tyrone. MacGiolla Martin was anglicised to Gilmartin. Giolla Earnáin O Martain (d. 1218) was an important bard and, later, there were two bishops of the name. The Martins of Connacht, the most prominent family of this name, claim descent from Olyver Martin, a Norman Crusader.

The Martins were one of the '14 Tribes of Galway' and they owned 200,000 acres in Connemara with an avenue of 30 miles to Ballynahinch Castle. Richard Martin's father had turned Protestant so that his son could sit in parliament and urge Catholic Emancipation. In his younger days Richard was known as 'Hairtrigger Dick' because of his constant duelling. This changed to 'Humanity Dick' when he got an act through parliament protecting animals and founded the Royal Society for the Prevention of Cruelty to Animals.

His granddaughter, Mary Laetitia, the 'Princess of Connemara', turned from a glittering success in London to care for her father's tenants during the Famine. He died from the famine fever and she died, penniless, aged 35, in the USA.

A kinswoman, Violet Martin of Ross, was Edith Somerville's collaborator in writing the *Experiences of an Irish RM*.

Edward Martyn of Tulira Castle founded the Feis Ceoil and became part of the Irish literary renaissance which included W.B. Yeats and George Moore.

The Martins who went to Australia produced a Prime Minister who held the post three times.

Moore *Ó Mórdha*

Moore, or in Irish Ó Mórdha, means 'noble'. They descend from Conal Cearnach, one of the chieftains of the legendary Knights of the Red Branch. Their territory was Leix, and in the Cistercian Abbey they founded is the tomb of their last chieftain, Malachi O More.

Today Moore is a common name, both in England and Ireland. There were also Moores who arrived with the Normans and it would be difficult now to disentangle the original Ó Mórdha and the Norman-English Moores.

The O Moores were a warrior people who defended their territory against the colonialists. In 1183 Conor O More defeated the Earl of Essex, sent by Queen Elizabeth to quell the Irish.

There are Moores who descend from an English soldier who had estates at Mellifont in Meath. About 1767 Field Marshal Sir Charles Moore, 6th Earl and 1st Marquess of Drogheda, built Moore Abbey in Kildare.

One of the earliest economists was an 18th-century Moore, while another Moor became John Wesley's right-hand man. The most celebrated is Thomas Moore, poet and musician.

Moore Hall in Connacht was the home of a distinguished line financed by wine trading with France. From here came the novelist and wit, George Moore. Brian Moore, formerly of Belfast, now in America, is a best-selling novelist.

Murphy *Ó Morchoe*

Ó Morchoe, or Murphy, the most numerous Irish name, means 'sea warrior'. There were several septs in Tyrone, Sligo and Wexford, where they were kings of Leinster. Dermot MacMurrough, the most famous Murphy, invited the Normans into Ireland. IIis brother, Murrough, is the eponymous ancestor of all the Wexford Murphys, including their present, accredited chieftain, 'The Ó Morchoe', who farms in Wexford.

Some of the Wexford sept moved west to Cork, where Daibhi Ó Murchu, the blind harper, played for Grace O Malley, the pirate queen. Seán Ó Murchadha was the last of the Blarney bards.

A singularly talented family, they have produced innumerable artists, sculptors, writers and a very famous actor and playwright, Arthur Murphy. Two heroic Wexford priests, both named Michael, lost their lives there in the 1798 rising.

One of the daughters of a shoemaker who emigrated to France, Marie Louise Murphy, was the French painter Boucher's favourite model until she became mistress to Louis XV.

Several branches of the Cork family who were brewers and distillers merged and, later, joined with Powers and Jamesons, the whiskey distillers. Irish Distillers Ltd, the biggest distillers in Ireland, still have Murphys on the board.

The Murphys in America are more numerous than in Ireland. They are also plentiful in Australia.

Nugent · *Nuinseann*

The name Nugent, originated in the 10th century in the French town of Nogent, from which the family moved to Ireland in the 12th century. They settled in Westmeath, where they were created Barons of Delvin, their principal stronghold. They formed new septs, one of which had its headquarters at Aghavarton Castle in Cork.

The Nugents are an outstanding military family. Some identified with the Irish while others held to the English rule, several acting as lord deputies.

Sir Christopher, 14th Baron Delvin, compiled *A Primer of the Irish Language* to help Elizabeth I understand the Irish. It did little good, for he spent much of his life imprisoned in Dublin Castle.

The term 'to nugentsize' originated with Robert Nugent, a poet, who made a nice life for himself by marrying wealthy widows, which craftily paved the way to a peerage from George III, to whom he loaned money.

Abroad the Nugents distinguished themselves in many wars. One fought at Fontenoy, another became a governor of Prague. Laval, Prince Count Nugent, field marshal and Knight of the Golden Fleece, is buried in his home at Fiume.

An illustrious exception was Christopher Nugent of Meath, who followed medicine and contributed to the cure of hydrophobia.

Ballinlough Castle in Westmeath is one of the fine houses still in Nugent occupation.

Many members of this family have settled in Canada.

O Brien

The O Briens take their name from the 10th-century Brian Boru who was High King of Ireland. A very powerful and numerous sept in Clare and Limerick, they spread far and wide and still predominate in Munster. Their history fills volumes, beginning with the saga of their contentions with the Normans and the Tudors. They were granted many titles of nobility; Earls of Thomond, Viscounts Clare, Earls of Inchiquin.

The 6th Earl of Thomond, 'Murrough of the Burnings', earned his second title for his siding with the Cromwellians in the ravaging. Repenting years later, he journeyed to Rome to expunge his atrocities.

Other more constructive Earls of Thomond built abbeys and fine castles, including Dromoland.

In the Battle of the Boyne they were active on both sides, the losing O Briens (the Viscounts Clare) fleeing to France where they founded Clare's Dragoons.

In Ireland by the 18th century they were parliamentarians, urging legislative independence for Ireland. Foremost among these was William Smith O Brien of Dromoland, whose nationalist views included the taking up of arms which led to his banishment for a while to Australia.

A number of O Briens chose the sea. The 3rd Marquis of Thomond was an admiral in the British navy. Captain Jeremiah O Brien and several of his brothers were in the American navy at the time of the revolution and it was they who opened the naval hostilities by capturing several of the English ships.

O Byrne *Ó Broin*

Byrne

With or without the O prefix, Byrne counts as one of the most numerous Irish names. Ó Broin, the Irish version, comes from Branach (raven), a son of Maolmordha, 11th-century King of Leinster. Kildare was Ó Broin country until they were driven south to the mountains of Wicklow by the encroaching Anglo-Normans.

They settled in Crioch Bhranach (O Byrne's Country), with Ballinacor as their headquarters. Their warrior chieftain, Fiach MacHugh O Byrne, followed the O Byrne tradition, waging guerrilla warfare against the English. Later, he was killed and his head was impaled outside Dublin Castle. A collection of poetry eulogising the O Byrnes, *Leabhar Branach*, is in the library of Trinity College Dublin.

Joining the exodus in 1691 they went to France, where they served in the army. Because of their aristocratic lineage a number of them were imprisoned and guillotined in Paris during the Revolution. O Byrnes were among the leading citizens of Bordeaux, where one family had a vineyard.

There were distinguished O Byrne bishops and surgeons in the USA. Donn-Byrne, the novelist, born in New York, returned to Ireland where he wrote patriotic Irish novels which had great success.

Gay Byrne is a well known Irish television personality.

The O Beirnes, whose territory is Connacht, are a completely distinct sept from the O Byrnes.

O Callaghan   *Ó Ceallacháin*

This name probably came from Ceallachan, 10th-century King of Munster and chieftain of the Eoghanact (a consortium of the leading families of Munster). Ceallachain means 'strife', which aptly describes this King of Munster who led plundering expeditions to the surrounding counties. He is also famed for killing Cinncide, father of the future king Brian Boru.

Just before the devastations of Cromwell, Colonel Donogh O Callaghan was a member of the Irish Confederation of Kilkenny. He was outlawed and had to seek refuge in France.

In the 18th century Cornelius O Callaghan of Tipperary was created Baron Lismore, one of the rare native Irishmen to be so honoured.

Father Jeremiah O Callaghan travelled through England and Europe vehemently preaching justice. In north America, where he finally settled, he was affectionately known as the 'Apostle of Vermont'.

In the 19th century in New York Edmund Bailey O Callaghan, a scholarly doctor, published a comprehensive *History of New York* — the first of its kind. The *History of the Irish Brigades in the Service of France* by John Cornelius O Callaghan is a thorough documentation of the 'Wild Geese' and their posterity.

Many Callaghans settled in Spain. Don Juan O Callaghan, a Barcelona lawyer, is the authenticated chief of his name.

O Connell *Ó Conaill*

The O Connells boast a pedigree dating back to a High King c. 280 BC. The name appears to have evolved from the ancient British or Celtic first name, Cunovalos.

The O Connells came from several distinct septs sited in Derry, Galway and Munster. Their chieftains had their castle at Ballycarberry near Cahirciveen. When it was broken up by the Cromwellians they began their long association with France and Austria. They were of a distinctively military cast.

When Muircheartach O Connell joined the Austrian army he changed his name, understandably, to Moritz. The Empress Maria Theresa appointed him Imperial Chamberlain. His kinsman, Count Daniel O Connell, had fought with the Prussians against Maria Theresa.

Another kinsman, Sir Maurice O Connell, was transferred at the time of the Revolution from the French to the British army. He was given a command in Australia, where he married the daughter of Captain Bligh of *The Bounty*.

Daniel Charles Count O Connell served in many armies. In France he was admitted to the nobility but had to flee the Revolution. His nephew was the 'Liberator', Daniel O Connell of Cahirciveen, a lawyer and orator, who roused the people to demand — and get — Catholic Emancipation.

The many O Connell scholars and clerics have been somewhat eclipsed by the soldiers and politicians. Father Daniel O Connell, a kinsman of the 'Liberator' and a Jesuit, is recognised internationally as an astronomer and seismologist.

O Connor *Ó Conchobhair*

O Conor

The O Connors hold pedigrees going back to the 2nd century. Conchobhair, meaning 'hero' or 'champion', was the 10th-century King of Connacht from whom they took their name. There were, however, at least six O Conor septs, not necessarily in the same line as Conchobhair. Among these were O Conor of Corcomroe in Clare, O Connor Faly of Offaly, O Connor Kerry, chief of the Munster O Connors, and O Connor Keenaght of Ulster. The O Conors of Connacht were the royal and predominant line. In the 12th century Turlough Mór O Conor was High King of Ireland.

Their family mansion, Clonalis near Roscommon, is a unique treasury of Irish relics and archives which have been professionally classified. When others fled from colonial oppression, the O Conors remained in their remote Belanagare fastness, the Connacht family seat which preceded Clonalis. The chiefs of this family style themselves O Conor Don.

In the 18th century there was a succession of O Conor scholars and antiquarians who collected and translated Irish manuscripts, many now in the Royal Irish Academy.

Space does not allow for a proper account of the eminent O Connors, among them writers, artists, soldiers, priests, politicians and diplomats. There was a Napoleonic general and a general with Simon Bolivar, a physician to the King of Poland, a governor of Zambia and another of Civita Vecchia, and a Charles O Connor of New York who declined an offer for presidency of the USA in the 19th century.

O Donnell *Ó Domhnaill*

The O Donnells are one of the eminent families whose forefather was Niall of the Nine Hostages. Tirconnell, meaning 'Connell's territory' (now Donegal) was their base, and from Domhnaill (world mighty) they took their name. Their chieftains were inaugurated on the Rock of Doon near Letterkenny.

Theirs is a history of battle. They built strongholds around Donegal and defended them first from their neighbours, the O Neills, and then, in a losing battle, from the Tudors.

As a youth the O Donnell heir, the great Red Hugh, was abducted and imprisoned in Dublin Castle. His escape through the snow-covered Wicklow mountains is one of the great sagas. He was a leader in the triumphant battle of the Yellow Ford, but died in Spain following the exodus after Kinsale.

The O Donnells established an Austrian line with a Major General Henry, Count O Donnell. Count Joseph, his son, was finance minister following Napoleon's depredations. Another O Donnell count was aide-de-camp to the Emperor Franz Josef. Their kinsmen reached the highest rank in Spain — Prime Minister in 1858.

Many O Donnells have been illustrious churchmen, including the 'Apostle of Newfoundland' and Cardinal Peter O Donnell in Ireland. Their present chieftain is a Franciscan missionary whose heir will come from the Duke of Tetuan's family in Spain. Clan rallies are held at intervals. The next is due in Donegal in 1985.

O Donovan *Ó Donnabhain*

The O Donovan pedigree goes back to Callaghan, a 10th-century King of Munster. From his son, Donnabhain, came the family name (donn meaning 'brown' and dubhann meaning 'black').

A noble race in Munster, they were chieftains in Carbery. Their extensive territory followed Limerick's River Maigue. Brugh Riogh ('royal residence') was the explanatory name of their stronghold until the Normans drove them south to Cork where they acquired more possessions and are still very numerous.

Because of their adherence to the doomed Stuarts they were outlawed and lost their wealth. In France, where they found careers in the army, O Donovan's Infantry was a regiment to be reckoned with. Because they were aristocrats they suffered sadly during the French Revolution.

Another O Donovan family of Kilkenny who claimed descent from Eoghan, a 3rd-century King of Munster, produced one of the most celebrated historians, John O Donovan. He published an *Irish Grammar* and translated and edited the first complete edition of the *Annals of the Four Masters*.

Jeremiah O Donovan, the revered patriot O Donovan Rossa (red), emigrated to America, driven out by his Fenian activities.

The classic short story writer, Frank O Connor was, in fact, born Michael O Donovan of Cork city.

Weight throwing was a Gaelic sport 3,000 years ago. In the last century an O Donovan in America was world and USA champion.

O Farrell *Ó Fearghaill*

More O Ferrall

Ó Fearghaill means 'man of great valour', an auspicious sobriquet inherited from a Lord of Annaly of the family which also named the town of Longford where their base was Longphuirt Ui Fhearghaill (O Farrell's Fort).

The O Farrells multiplied and divided into two septs; O Farrell Boy (buidhe means 'yellow') and O Farrell Bán (bán means 'white'). In the *Annals of the Four Masters* they are accorded much space.

When they married into the Moore family they founded their own illustrious sept — the More O Ferralls.

Many went to Europe; one was a Spanish diplomat; another was a Major General in the Austrian army. Several O Farrells were in the service of the King of Sardinia until he was overthrown by Napoleon.

Richard More Ó Ferrall, MP, Lord of the Treasury, First Secretary to the Admiralty and the first civilian governor of Malta, gave up this glittering career in 1850, disagreeing with the Prime Minister's opposition to the liberalisation of Catholicism in England.

For decades the BBC and the British film and television industry were dominated by George More O Ferrall, who had studied acting before becoming joint producer of the first television programme ever made. He later directed many films and plays.

Of the two branches of the More O Ferrall family one was based at Balyna, Kildare, originally the Moore family home. The other, at Kildangan near Monasterevan, Kildare, is celebrated for its rare gardens and blood stock.

O Flaherty *Ó Flaithbheartaigh*

The O Flahertys boast a genealogy going back at least 3,000 years. They were sea-faring people of Connacht and in earlier days they were the enemies of the elitist '14 Tribes of Galway', who dubbed them 'the Ferocious O Flahertys'. They carried on a continuous warfare against their neighbours, the Burkes, and the royal O Conors. In time they defeated the Burkes and acquired much territory between Lough Corrib and the Atlantic, where they were styled Lords of Iar (West) Connacht. Aughnanure Castle near Oughterard, Galway, is a majestic ruin tinged with stories of bloody O Flaherty revenge killings.

The pirate Queen Granuaile (*see* O Malley) had, as her first husband, Donal an Chogaidh (of the battles) O Flaherty, but he succumbed early to his lust for battle. The last O Flaherty chieftain, Roderick of Moycullen, died in a miserable cabin but left an invaluable history written by himself.

During World War II the 'Scarlet Pimpernel of the Vatican' was a Kerry O Flaherty priest who helped allied soldiers to escape from German-occupied Italy.

The O Flaherty prowess in modern times is celebrated in Liam O Flaherty, novelist, playwright, short story writer and formerly, man of Aran. Robert Flaherty, son of an Irish emigré, made documentary films in the USA including *Man of Aran*.

In Ulster a different form of Irish is spoken, which accounts for O Flaherty, who was styled Lord of Aileach in Donegal, having his name transformed to O Laverty.

O Grady *Ó Grádaigh*

Ó Grádaigh means 'illustrious' and their pedigree shows the O Gradys to be of Dalcassian sept, kinsmen of the royal O Briens. Their territories circled Clare and they had their fortress on Inis Cealtra (Holy Island) on Lough Derg. A ruined O Grady castle testifies to their settlements in Clare, as does Lough O Grady near Scarriff.

Their neighbours, the O Briens, dispersed them to Limerick, where the present chief of the name, Lieutenant Colonel Gerard Vigors de Courcy O Grady, lives at Killballyowen.

During the frenetic period of Henry VIII's rule an O Grady changed his faith and his name to the less Irish sounding Brady in order to keep his lands. His son was the first Protestant Bishop of Meath.

The family has long since reverted to its original name. Darby O Grady, who lost his lands during another penal purge, had them restored to him following his marriage to Sir Thomas Standish's daughter. In gratitude, there has been a male or female Standish in succeeding generations of the family until the present day.

A Standish O Grady who was an Attorney General was created Viscount Guillamore. His nephew was the distinguished Standish O Grady, engineer in America and then, on his return to Ireland, a most remarkable antiquarian and compiler of Irish manuscripts. Another Standish O Grady was the famous writer of heroic Irish folk stories. In America an O Grady, married to a black American lady, was the great grandfather of Cassius Clay, alias Muhammed Ali.

O Keeffe *Ó Caoimh*

Art O Caom, son of Fionghuine, the King of Munster who died in 902, gave his name to the O Keeffes whose territory was around Glanmore and Fermoy in Cork. When they were uprooted by the Normans they moved south to the Duhallow county where their surroundings came to be called Pobble O Keeffe (O Keeffe country). Caom means 'noble' or 'gentle'.

Their celebrated poet, Owen O Keeffe, who was president of the Cork bards, was also a parish priest of Doneraile.

Following the submergence of the old Gaelic order, the O Keeffes began to feature in the army lists in France. There were many O Keeffe officers, and as they settled in France their name was gradually eroded to Cuif.

Those who managed to survive at home were able to use their talents with the easing of the penal laws. One artist O Keeffe, following training in Dublin, got the signature of approval in London with an exhibition at the Royal Academy.

His brother, John, was an actor and dramatist. When he first went to London his name lacked the O prefix, as was usual then. As a successful playwright and song writer he gained the confidence to show his Irish origins by returning the O to Keeffe.

When John Lanigan of Tipperary married an O Keeffe heiress they combined their names. The Lanigan O Keeffe families have a definite legal tradition. Some have gone to Australia, others to Rhodesia, now Zimbabwe.

O Kelly *Ó Ceallaigh*

The O Kellys derive their name from Ceallach, a celebrated 9th-century chieftain. Ceallach, meaning 'war' or 'contention', was at one time an apt cognomen for the O Kellys who, after the Murphys, have the most numerous name in Ireland.

For centuries their territories included much of Galway and Roscommon, known as 'O Kelly's Country'. At one time the O Kellys had become so prolific they spread out into eight different septs.

In 1351 the O Kelly chief invited all the musicians and poets to spend Christmas with him — a gesture which originated the expression 'O Kelly's Welcome'. Murtough O Kelly, the Archbishop of Tuam who compiled the historic *Book of the O Kellys*, was one of many distinguished O Kelly churchmen. Malachy O Kelly led the horrendous inter-tribal massacre at Knocktoe in 1499 when the leading Irish families fought each other.

The O Kellys who fled with the 'Wild Geese' were distinguished in the Irish regiments of France. The enduring dynasty who were honoured with the title Count of the Holy Roman Empire began when the Austrian Empress Maria Theresa conferred it on Dillon John Kelly.

The ballad 'Kelly the Boy from Killann' refers to a Kelly killed in the 1798 rising in Wexford. Sean Kelly, of Carrick-on-Suir, continues to win awards as an international cyclist. The much-lamented Grace of Monaco was a Kelly from America, where there are far more Kellys than in Ireland. Not the least of their representatives in Australia was the gangster Ned Kelly.

O Kennedy *Ó Cinneide*

There is a Kennedy clan in Scotland also who, very far back, may have been related to the Irish Kennedys. They were certainly kinsmen of King Brian Boru, from whose brother, Dunchad, they descend. Cean Éidig, which means 'ugly head', was the father of Brian and Dunchad and it is from him that the name originated.

For a long time the O Kennedys were settled in Clare, near Killaloe. The O Briens and the MacNamaras drove them away to Tipperary and Kilkenny, then known as Ormond. For 400 years they were Lords of Ormond and grew so mighty they divided into several new septs. For a long time they held out against the Butler-led encroachment of the Normans. These stirring times are recorded in the *Ormond Deeds,* (c. 1579), which were presented to John F. Kennedy during his 1963 visit.

By c. 1746 the combination of the Butlers and Cromwellians had deprived them of their 20,000 acres and their castles. They flocked to France to join the Irish Brigades. In Spain their name was adapted to Quenedy.

In the 19th and 20th centuries the Kennedys have been distinguished in the church, medicine, the law and the navy. There was a popular songwriter too: Jimmy Kennedy of 'Red Sails in the Sunset' fame. The Kennedy Road crossing from Simla to Tibet commemorates the engineer who built it.

Towering over all are the Kennedys who sailed from Dunganstown to Boston, from whom sprang John F. Kennedy, President of the USA.

O Mahony *Ó Mahúna*

The O Mahony name comes from Mathghamhan, son of Cian Mac Mael Muda, a 10th-century prince and his wife, Sadbh, who was the High King Brian Boru's daughter. They were of the Eoghanacht, a regal dynasty of Munster.

Their Munster possessions were vast. They sprinkled their 14 castles all around the Cork coast, west to Mizen Head. Many of their descendants are still there, many more scattered into new septs or emigrated.

In the courts of Europe they held distinguished military and diplomatic appointments and married into the nobility. Their chief representative in France to-day is the Vicomte Yves O Mahony of Orleans.

Colonel John O Mahony was a scholar whose nationalism forced him to emigrate to America, where he promoted the revolutionary Fenian cause. During the Civil War his Fenians served in the 99th Regiment of New York, of which he was colonel.

The celebrated 'Father Prout' who wrote the poem 'The Bells of Shandon' was in fact Francis Mahony, son of a woollen manufacturing family in Blarney. Dave Allen, the television comedian, was born David Tynan O Mahony, son of a Dublin journalist. 'The Pope' O Mahony, one of Dublin's best loved characters and a Cork barrister, raised genealogy to an art, weaving it into his speeches and broadcasts.

The very numerous O Mahonys are well served by a professional genealogical association which has held a rally in a different O Mahony castle every year for 30 years.

O Malley *Ó Máille*

Melia

The O Malleys are a very old Mayo family whose name is said to derive from the Celtic word for chief (maglios). For many centuries they were chieftains of the baronies of Burrishoole and Murrisk, where the sea was their chief occupation.

One of the most remarkable women in Irish history, Grace O Malley, (known as Granuaile) was the daughter of the O Malley chieftain Owen. As a mere 15-year-old she was married to an O Flaherty. When he was killed in battle she married a Burke. She frequently contended with the marauding English, both by land and by the sea from which she got her living. She was captured several times and was rescued from the gallows. In her old age, 'as a princess and equal', she visited Queen Elizabeth in London.

With the breakdown of the ancient chieftaincies the O Malleys disappeared abroad. Charles O Malley and his five brothers gave their lives to a diversity of armies. It was said, 'none of his family were ever known to follow any trade or profession but arms, earning no fortune to replace what had been taken from them'.

The O Malleys produced many high churchmen and one unorthodox priest, Thaddeus O Malley, who was returned from America because of his progressive religious and political views.

Ernest O Malley, a veteran of the Civil War, wrote a vivid autobiography entitled *On Another Man's Wound*.

Melia is sometimes found as a variant of O Malley.

O Neill

The name is the same in Irish as in English and for 1,000 years O Neill has been one of the most prestigious of Irish families. Niall means 'champion' and was first used by Domhnall, grandson of Nial Glun Dubh (black knee), King of Ireland, killed in 890 by the Norsemen. The O Neills go further back, claiming descent from the legendary Niall of the Nine Hostages.

They were very strong in Ulster, and to curb their power Queen Elizabeth had their Tullahogue inauguration stone broken up. In the 14th century they separated into two main branches; the senior branch were Princes of Tyrone while the junior branch were the Clanaboys of Antrim and Down.

Shane's Castle in Antrim is now a splendid show place, managed by Raymond, 4th Lord O Neill, a descendant of the Chichesters who adopted their maternal O Neill name.

Terence O Neill was Prime Minister of Northern Ireland from 1963-9. The O Neill pedigree is well looked after by the Irish Genealogical Association in Belfast which, in 1983, organised a big clan gathering. Jorge O Neill—his family have long been resident in Portugal—is the present representative of the Clanaboys. The Tyrone branch is extinct — or missing.

Eugene O Neill, the New York dramatist, and the politician 'Tip' O Neill are just two of the celebrated representatives of this great family in the USA.

O Reilly *Ó Raghailligh*

The O Reillys are thought to be kinsmen of the O Conor kings of Connacht through Maolmordha (Myles), whose great grandson was Ragheallach (gregarious race), from whom the O Reillys took their name. Their territory was around Lough Oughter in Cavan and as they increased they extended their families and their territory, particularly to Westmeath.

Cathal O Reilly, Prince of Breffny, founded the monastery on Lough Oughter in 1237 and, later, Cavan's Franciscan Abbey was founded by Giolla Iosa O Reilly. There were 39 O Reilly abbots and five held the primacy of Armagh as well as several bishoprics. They were also kinsmen of St Oliver Plunkett.

The celebrated Count Alexander O Reilly from Meath distinguished himself first in the Austrian service and then in the Spanish army. He put down a rebellion in Louisiana where he became governor. O Reilly pedigrees are found in Havana, as are many of their titled descendants. The O Reilly papers and portraits in Trinity College Dublin were donated by a descendant of Colonel Myles O Reilly, an officer in the Irish cavalry in 1641 who fled to Spain.

The O Reillys have a reputation as astute financiers. In the 15th century they devised their own coinage. A 'Reilly' has come to signify a coin of useful value. In the 20th century an O Reilly continues to head the family industry now amalgamated with the Irish Distillers Group (formerly John Power and Sons). Tony O Reilly, one time Irish rugby international, is chief executive of the American Heinz company as well as a number of companies in Ireland.

O Rourke *Ó Ruairc*

O Rourke is thought to have come from the Norse name Hrothrekr. These Norsemen stayed to integrate thoroughly and to produce three Kings of Connacht. Styled Lords of Breffny, their chieftains ruled territory in Cavan and Leitrim, where their stronghold was at Dromahair on Lough Gill. In the O Rourke pedigree there are 19 chieftains, all named Tiernan. Of these, the most notorious was the Tiernan who ravaged Meath and invaded Connacht where Dermot MacMurrough (see Kavanagh), the King of Leinster, was also foraging. Dermot MacMurrough abducted Tiernan's wife, Dervorgilla, earning his undying hatred. When Tiernan allied himself with the O Conor King of Connacht they deposed Dermot, who went to England to seek help. Thus began the Anglo-Norman invasion. Tiernan was slain by the Norman Hugo de Lacy.

Following the confiscation of their land by the Crown, the O Rourkes headed for Europe, where they distinguished themselves in a variety of exalted positions. There were many O Rourke bishops of Killala, including one who became chaplain to the Austrian court. The Empress Maria Theresa had two Owen O Rourkes in her service, one of whom was her ambassador to the exiled Stuarts at Vienna.

Count John O Rourke, Prince of Breffny, served the Russian Tsar and then the French, who made him a count. His nephew was the famous General Count Iosif Kornilievich O Rourke, who took part in the defeat of Napoleon. His portrait is in the Hermitage in Leningrad, where there are many O Rourke records. O Rourke descendants still live in Russia and Poland.

O Sullivan *Ó Súileabháin*

In Irish Súileabháin means 'one' or maybe, 'hawk-eyed'. Their ancestry is from Olioll Olum, the 3rd-century King of Munster who was progenitor of the great Eoganacht clan. Tipperary was the first O Sullivan territory, and as they multiplied they spread to Cork and Kerry. The senior chieftain, O Sullivan Mór, had his stronghold at Kenmare Bay in Kerry. O Sullivan Beare occupied Dunboy on Bantry Bay.

The O Sullivans fought at Kinsale and defended Dunboy to the last stone. Then began O Sullivan Beare's epic march. In January 1602, with 400 soldiers and 600 civilians, they walked 200 miles north in two weeks of bitter cold and savage attacks to reach Brian O Rourke's Leitrim Castle. Only 35 had survived, including one woman. Although Elizabeth was dead, James I was no friend of the Irish. O Sullivan Beare and his family left for the hospitality of Philip III of Spain, where many of his family gave distinguished service in the army and navy.

In the 18th and 19th centuries there was a remarkable flowering of literary talent. Owen Roe O Sullivan, teacher, sailor and womanizer, is now acknowledged to be a great lyric poet.

In France, during the Revolution, an O Sullivan was one of the chief tyrants, sinking barges full of priests and aristocrats to bypass the slowness of the guillotine!

Sir Arthur O Sullivan was the musical half of the Gilbert and Sullivan operas.

O Toole *Ó Tuathail*

O Toole comes from Tuathal, a 10th-century King of Leinster, of which province they were one of the great septs. Some scholars say tuathal means 'mighty people', while others think it means 'prosperous'. Although they originated from Kildare, the O Tooles are universally associated with Wicklow, where they built their castles and from which they set out to attack their neighbours and, later, the English.

When he was a young boy Laurence O Toole was captured by Dermot MacMurrough (*see* Kavanagh) who had killed his grandfather. When released, Laurence found his vocation in the monastic settlement at Glendalough. In 1161 he was appointed first Irish Archbishop of Dublin. A great church reformer and an intermediary between the Anglo-Normans and the Irish, he died at Eu on his way to plead with King Henry in Normany. In 1220 he was canonised and is patron saint of Dublin.

Laurence O Toole, one of the many O Tooles who fled abroad to join the Irish Brigades, had eight sons in the French army. His son, Colonel John O Toole, is the progenitor of the present Count of Limoges in France. Luke of Toole helped Princess Clementina to escape from Innsbruck to marry Prince Charles Stuart.

There were several O Toole septs in Ulster and Connacht. In Monaghan and Dundalk Toal and Toole are easily recognisable as stemming from O Toole.

Plunkett

The Plunketts—the name comes from a French word for blonde — are an aristocratic family who came to Ireland via Denmark before the Normans, and integrated well by marrying. They held spacious territories in Meath and Louth. In the early 1600s they were accorded a variety of titles. Randal Plunkett, 19th Baron Dunsany, farms his big estate in Meath. His nearby Kinsman, Oliver Plunkett, 19th Earl of Fingall, the last of his line, died in 1984. The 17th Lord Louth lives in the Channel Islands.

The Plunketts fought for the doomed Catholic Stuarts, fleeing with them to France to join the Irish regiments. In the 18th century, to save their lands, they conformed to the established religion. When religious persecution eased most returned to their original faith.

Their younger sons spread abroad to become British diplomats, admirals and soldiers. They were one of only two Irish families distinguished by a canonisation—Oliver Plunkett (1625-81). Ordained in Rome, he was Archbishop of Armagh and was martyred at Tyburn. In 1975 he was canonised in Rome, with his kinsman, Lord Dunsany, attending. He preserves the saint's crozier and ring in Dunsany Castle.

William Conyngham Plunket of Enniskillen, one of the finest speakers in the London House of Commons, was the 1st Baron Plunket. His grandson, also William Conyngham, 4th Baron Plunket, was Church of Ireland Archbishop of Dublin.

Power
de Paor

When the Powers came to Ireland with the Normans they were known as le Poer, meaning 'poor'. Maybe this had something to do with a vow of poverty they had taken at one time. They were certainly not poor, for they owned estates in Wicklow and in Waterford, where, as Marquesses of Waterford, they continue to maintain Curraghmore House (once described as the 'Versailles of Ireland').

Margaret Power, who married the Earl of Blessington, was known as 'the most beautiful Countess of Blessington'. When the Earl died, she and Count D'Orsay, the great dandy and painter, hosted a salon for the intellectuals of London — men only. The Earl had left no fortune. Soon she had to sell her London house and provide for herself and her improvident Limerick family. She wrote for ten hours a day, churning out books and articles until her death in Paris, where she had fled to escape her creditors.

William Grattan Tyrone Power of Waterford became a leading Irish actor on the English stage. Tyrone Power, the film star and romantic hero, was his great grandson. Another great grandson was Sir Tyrone Guthrie, theatre and television producer, and director of the Old Vic and Sadler's Wells theatres.

Sir James Power founded Powers Distillery in Dublin in 1791. His firm invented the famous 'Baby Power' miniature liquor bottle.

Regan *Ó Reagáin*

Regan is a widespread name which came, not from one ancestor, but from several. There were Ó Riagáins in Meath and Dublin. They were important because they were of the 'Four Tribes of Tara'. They were very active against the Scandinavian invaders but lost their importance with the arrival of the Normans who drove them away to Leix.

The other and in no way related sept were descended from one of Brian Boru's brothers, Donnchadh. They were all of the powerful Dalcassian sept which ruled in counties Clare, Leinster and Tipperary.

Maurice O Regan, who was born about 1125, wrote a history concerning the arrival of the Normans. As a kind of diplomatic secretary to Dermot MacMurrough (see Kavanagh), King of Leinster, he was well positioned to give a first-hand account.

Reagans emigrated to the USA before the Famine. There was a Reagan Surgeon with Corcoran's Irish Legion. Another Reagan, a progressive jurist in Texas, was, at one time, Confederate Post Master. A Democrat, he lost popularity at the end of the Civil War because he advocated civil rights for negroes.

Ronald Reagan is one of the many distinguished descendants of Brian Boru. His grandfather emigrated from Ballyporeen, Tipperary, to London and later to Illinois. In Ireland Regan is pronounced Reegan, but genealogists agree that 'Raygan', as pronounced by Ronald Reagan, is correct for the sept from which he sprang.

Roche   *de Róiste*

It is thought the Roches originated in Flanders. They certainly arrived in Ireland with the Normans from Roch Castle, their Pembrokeshire fortress. Their name comes from this castle. They multiplied to become five different branches.

David Roche, who was created 1st Viscount Fermoy in 1570, was an ancestor of Princess Diana of Wales. The 8th Viscount Roche was one of the leaders in the rebellion of 1641. His wife, Lady Roche (née Power), was hanged for trying to defend Castletownroche. Her husband fled to join the Flemish army.

Maurice Roche, Mayor of Cork in the reign of Elizabeth I, was given his gold chain by her for his help in suppressing the rebel Earl of Desmond (*see* FitzGerald).

The Roches had many good churchmen, including a bishop of Ferns. They also had 'characters' such as the ferocious 'Tiger' Roche, a dandy who tricked innocent heiresses out of their fortunes and was too quick with his fists. His brother, the politician Boyle Roche, was notorious for his Irish 'bulls', particularly one that is still quoted: 'Why should we do anything for posterity — what has posterity ever done for us?'

In Ireland, Liam de Roiste, an Irish scholar and a member of the Gaelic League, took part in the fight for independence and sat in Daíl Éireann.

From the 1960s until comparatively recently the Roches used to hold an annual rally in one of their surviving castles. Perhaps this will be revived?

Ryan *Ó Maoilriain*

Mulryan

The Ryans formed their name from an old personal name which could mean either 'administrator' or 'water'. Descending from a 2nd-century King of Leinster, Cathaoir Mór, the clan became very numerous and separated into two main branches. The Ó Riains of Idrone in Carlow and the Ó Maoilriains, who were chiefs in Owney around Tipperary and Limerick.

Following the Treaty of Limerick the Ryans went abroad. A Captain Luke Ryan commanded a French privateer during the American War of Independence. Juan Francesco O Ryan was an admiral and a minister in Chile. Descendants of Field Marshal Tomás O Ryan are still in Spain.

A family of Thady Ryans of Knocklong, Limerick, have been famous for centuries for their horses and their Scarteen Hounds. The present Thady Ryan has been chef d'équipe of the Irish Olympic team several times.

Journalists, editors and novelists have enhanced the Ryan name, among them Desmond Ryan, biographer and novelist, A.P. Ryan, editor of the London *Times* and Cornelius Ryan, who wrote the best-seller *The Longest Day*.

Many Ryans distinguished themselves in Australia and the USA, where Thomas Fortune Ryan, a penniless orphan, fulfilled the American dream by becoming a multi-millionaire known as the 'noiseless man of American finance'.

Sheridan *Ó Sirideáin*

The origins of the Sheridans is obscure. Their name was, at first, a personal name, and Cavan was their territory. Literature was their abiding talent, but they were also good churchmen, including one who helped the Provost of Trinity College Dublin to translate the Bible into Irish.

Thomas predominates in the Sheridan pedigree. There was the Thomas who was a close friend of James II, with whom he fled into exile. Thomas, his son, was one of the famous 'Seven Men of Moidart' and took part in the decisive battle of Culloden. Many were graduates of Trinity College Dublin, such as Thomas, a notable scholar and friend of Dean Swift of St Patrick's Cathedral. His son, Thomas, was manager of the Theatre Royal Dublin and was also a very good actor.

Thomas's second son, Richard Brinsley Sheridan, became the most successful dramatist of his day; *The Rivals* and *School for Scandal* are among his best known plays. His son Thomas was a short-lived poet whose wife was a novelist.

Joseph Sheridan Le Fanu (his mother was a Sheridan, his father a Huguenot) wrote enthralling tales of the supernatural.

Margaret Burke Sheridan broke the literary mould. She was an opera singer who lived in Italy and was a leading member of Milan's La Scala Theatre.

General Philip Sheridan's roots were in Cavan. He distinguished himself during the American Civil War at the battle for the Shenandoah Valley. His famous 20-mile ride is part of American folk history.

Taaffe

David is the Welsh equivalent of Taaffe, and the family came from Wales in 1196 to settle in Louth.

Smarmore Castle, near Ardee, is still in Taffe possession. There were a number of Taaffes in the church, and a few eccentrics, including a priest who forged a Papal Bull giving him leave to do what he thought fit with the church in Ireland!

From earliest days the Taaffes were statesmen and soldiers. A Taaffe of Ballymote Castle in Sligo fought against the Irish at Kinsale and was duly rewarded with a knighthood.

Theobald, 2nd Viscount Taaffe, differing from his grandfather, joined the Catholic Confederacy at Kilkenny and commanded the Connacht forces against Cromwell.

Nicholas, 6th Viscount Taaffe, was a Lieutenant General in the Austrian army and chancellor to the king. He introduced the Irish potato to Silesia. He lived to be 92 in his Bohemian castle Elischau, today a Czechoslovakian military school.

Edward, 11th Viscount Taaffe, Baron of Ballymote, was Prime Minister of Austria for 14 years. Following the mysterious suicide of the Hapsburg heir, Prince Rudolph, Count Taaffe and his heirs were entrusted with the documents relating to the investigation.

Count Eduard Taaffe came to Ireland in the 1930s and was offered enormous sums to sell the Hapsburg papers. He declined and placed them in the Vatican archives.

The Taaffes are numerous in Ireland, on the land, in the professions and especially in horsebreeding.

Walsh *Breathnach*

Walsh was the name used to designate the hundreds of Welshmen who accompanied the Normans to Ireland. Consequently there is no common Walsh ancestor for this family.

Philip and his brother, David, who arrived in the 12th century, are supposed to be progenitors of the Walshes of Dublin, Kilkenny, Leix, Waterford and Wicklow. They are recorded plentifully in Burke's and other genealogical sources, sometimes with a final 'e' to the name. Others altered their name to Breathnach, the Irish for Welshman.

They were prominent in the church, both Catholic and Protestant. Nicholas, Bishop of Ossory about 1567, had his church services printed in Irish to help convert the 'papists'.

Peter Walsh, a Franciscan and a very contentious religious, suffered excommunication — he opposed the papal nuncio and repudiated papal infallability.

When Cromwell's soldiers planted Clonmel, Tipperary, the only Walsh left in the town was John, who had acted as Cromwell's loyal adviser.

Antoine Vincent Walshe, son of a Waterford shipbuilder, commanded the ship which landed Prince Charles Stuart in Scotland in 1745. His eldest son was the founder of the Counts Walsh de Serrant, who are still in France. A kinsman was Superior of the Irish College in Paris.

Maurice Walsh of Kerry, who spent many years in the customs service in Scotland, wrote a host of bestsellers, one of which, *The Quiet Man,* was made into a popular film.

A Short List of
Other Prominent Names

Unless otherwise stated, all these names are derived from family personal names. Their meaning is given wherever it is possible to discover it.

Barrett, *Báróid:* Norman, Cork, Mayo, Galway.

Brady, *MacBrádaigh:* 'spirited', Ulster, Leinster, Cavan.

Breen, *O Braoin:* 'sadness', 'sorrow', Kilkenny, Wexford, Westmeath.

Brennan, *O Braonáin:* 'little drop', Kilkenny, Kerry, Westmeath.

Buckley, *O Buachalla:* 'boy', Cork, Kerry.

Carey, *O Ciardha:* Kildare, Kerry.

Cassidy, *O Caiside:* Fermanagh originally, now widespread.

Clancy, *MacFhlannchaidh:* 'ruddy warrior', Clare, Leitrim.

Coghlan, Coughlan, *MacCochlain* or *O Cochlain:* 'cape' or 'hood', Offaly, Cork.

Connolly, *O Conghaile:* 'Valorous', Connacht, Ulster, Monaghan, Cork.

Conroy, Mulconry, *O Conratha:* 'hound of prosperity', Roscommon, Clare.

Conway, *MacConnmhaigh:* Clare, Kerry, County Dublin.

Cooney, *O Cuanaic:* 'handsome', 'elegant', Galway, Clare, West Cork.

Corcoran, *O Corcrain:* 'ruddy', Fermanagh, Offaly, Mayo, Kerry.

Costello, Nangle, de Angulos, *MacOisdealbh:* 'son of Oistealb', Norman, Connacht, but widespread.

Crowley, *O Cruadhlaoich:* 'hunch-backed', Roscommon, Cork.

Cummins, *O Comáin:* 'a hurley', Mayo, Kerry, Limerick.

Curran, *O Corráin:* Ulster, Galway, Waterford, Kerry.

Delany, Delaney, *O Dubhshlaine;* 'of the river Slaney', Leix, Dublin.

Dempsey, *O Diomasaigh:* 'proud', Leix, Offaly.

Devine, *O Daimhin:* 'bard', 'poet', Fermanagh, Tyrone, Dublin, Cavan, Louth.

Devlin, *O Doibhlin:* Sligo, Tyrone.

Dolan, *O Dobhailen:* 'black defiance', 'challenge', Galway, Roscommon.

Doran, *O Deoradháin:* 'exile' or 'stranger', Down, Armagh, Leix, Wexford, Kerry.

Dowling, *O Dunlaing:* Leix, Kilkenny, Carlow, Wicklow, Dublin.

Duggan, *O Dubhagain:* 'black', Cork, Galway, Donegal, Tipperary.

Fagan, O Hagan, *O Faodhagain:* 'little Hugh', Kerry, Dublin.

Fahy, Fahey, *O Fathaigh:* 'field green', Galway, Tipperary.

Fallon, *O Fallamhain:* 'ruler', Galway, Donegal, Cork, Kerry, Wexford.

Fitzpatrick, *MacGiolla Padraig:* 'servant of St Patrick', Leix, widespread.

Flanagan, *O Flannagain:* 'red', Roscommon, Offaly, Fermanagh.

Flynn, *O Floinn;* 'red', 'ruddy', Cork, Roscommon, Antrim.

Fogarty, (cognate with Gogarty), *O Fogartaigh:* 'exiled', 'banished', Tipperary.

Foley, *O Foghladha:* 'plunderer', Waterford, mostly Munster.

Gaffney, *O Gamhna:* 'calf', Connacht.

Galvin, Gallivan, *O Gealbháin:* Kerry, Roscommon.

Garvey, *O Gairbith:* 'rough peace', Armagh, Down, Donegal.

Geraghty, *Mag Oireachtaigh:* 'court' or 'assembly', Roscommon, Galway.

Hickey, *O hIcidhe:* 'healer', Clare, Limerick, Tipperary.

Jennings, *MacSheóinín:* 'John' (originally Burkes), Connacht.

Kelleher, *O Céileachair:* 'loving spouse', Clare, Cork, Kerry.

Kinsella, *O Cinnsealach:* (originally Mac Murrough), Wexford, Wicklow.

Lalor, Lawlor, *O Leathlobhair:* 'half-leper', Leix.

Lee, *O Laoidhigh:* 'poetic', Tipperary, Galway, Cork, Limerick.

Lyons, Lehane, Lane, *O Laighin:* Galway.

MacAuley, *MacAmhlaoibh:* Fermanagh, Westmeath, Cork.

MacAuliffe, *MacAmhlaoibh:* Norse, 'Olaf', Cork.

MacBride, *MacGiolla Brighde:* 'son of the servant of St Brigid', Donegal.

MacCann, *MacAnnadh:* Armagh.

MacCormack, *MacCormaic:* all over Ireland.

MacElroy, *MacGiolla Rua:* 'red-haired youth', Fermanagh, Leitrim.

MacEvoy, *MacGuiollabhuidhe:* 'yellow lad', Louth, Leix.

MacGee, Magee, MacKee, *Mag Aodha:* Antrim, Down, Armagh.

MacGovern, Magauran, *Mag Samhrain:* 'summer', Cavan, Leitrim, Fermanagh.

MacHugh, *MacAoda:* Galway, Mayo, Leitrim, Donegal, Fermanagh.

MacInerney, *Mac an Airchinnigh:* 'steward of church lands', Connacht.

MacLoughlin, O Loghlen, *O Maoilsheachlainn:* Donegal, Meath, Clare.

MacManus, *MacMaghnuis:* Norse, 'Magnus', Fermanagh, Connacht.

MacNally, *Mac an Fhailghigh:* 'poor man', Mayo, Armagh, Monaghan.

MacNulty, *Mac an Ultaigh:* 'ulidian', 'of Ulster', also Mayo.

MacQuaid, *Mac Uaid:* 'Wat' or 'Walter', Ulster.

MacQuillan, *MacCoilin:* Norman, Ulster.

MacSweeney, *MacSuibhne:* 'Scottish mercenaries', Donegal, Cork.

Madden, *O Madáin:* 'small dog', Limerick, Longford, Galway, Offaly.

Maher, *O Meachair:* 'hospitable', Tipperary, Kilkenny.

Molloy, *O Maolmhudaidh:* 'noble chief', Offaly, widespread.

Moloney, *O Maoldhomhnaigh:* Clare, Tipperary.

Monahan, *O Manacháin:* 'monk', Roscommon.

Mooney, *O Maonaigh:* 'wealthy', Ulster, Offaly, Sligo.

Moran, *O Móráin:* 'great', Connacht.

Moriarty, *O Muircheartaigh:* 'expert navigator', Kerry.

Morrissey, *O Muirgheasa:* 'sea choice', Sligo, Waterford, Limerick, Cork.

Mulcahy, *O Maol Cataigh:* 'battle chief', Munster.

Mulligan, *O Maolagáin:* Donegal, Monaghan, Mayo.

Nolan, *O Nuaillain:* 'noble', 'famous', Carlow, West Cork.

O Casey, *O Cathasaigh:* 'vigilant', 'watchful', Munster.

O Dea, *O Deaghaidh:* Clare, Limerick, Tipperary, Cork, Dublin.

O Dowd, *O Dubhda:* 'black', Mayo, Sligo, Galway.

O Driscoll, *O hEidersceoil:* 'intermediary', Cork predominantly.

O Dwyer, *O Dubhuidir:* 'black odar', Sligo, Mayo.

O Flanagan, *O Flannagain:* 'red', Connacht.

O Gara, *O Gadhra:* 'a mastiff', Sligo, Mayo.

O Gorman, MacGorman, *O Gormain:* 'blue', Leix, Monaghan, Clare.

O Hagan, *O hAodhagain:* 'young', Tyrone.

O Halloran, *O hAllmhurain:* 'stranger beyond the sea', Clare, Galway.

O Hara, *O hEaghra:* Sligo, Antrim.

O Hegarty, *O hEigceartaigh:* 'unjust', Donegal, Derry, Cork.

O Higgins, *O hUigin:* 'knowledge', ingenuity', Sligo, Leinster, Munster.

O Leary, *O Laoghaire:* 'calf keeper', Cork.

O Meara, *O Meadhra:* 'mirth', Tipperary.

O Riordan, *O Riordáin:* 'royal bard', Tipperary, Cork.

O Shaughnessy, *O Seachnsaigh:* Galway, Clare, Limerick.

O Shea, *O Seaghada:* 'majestic', 'courteous', Kerry, Kilkenny.

Phelan, Whelan, *O Faoláin:* 'joyful', Waterford, Kilkenny, Wexford, Carlow.

Quigley, *O Coigligh:* 'untidy hair', Mayo, Donegal, Derry, Sligo, Galway.

Quinlan, *O Caoindealbháin:* 'gracefully shaped', Munster.

Quinn, *O Cuinn:* 'intelligent', Antrim, Longford, Clare.

Rafferty, *O Reachtaire:* Connacht.

Redmond, *Réamonn:* Norman, Wexford, Wicklow.

Rice, Welsh, *Rhys:* Kerry, Louth, Dublin, Ulster.

Rooney, *O Ruanaidh:* 'hero', Down, widespread.

Scanlan, *O Scannláin:* Kerry, Limerick, Cork, also Connacht.

Scully, *O Scolaidhe:* 'crier', Tipperary, Leinster.

Shannon, *O Seanacháin:* 'old', 'wise', Clare, Ulster.

Sheehan, *O Siodhacáin:* 'peaceful', Munster.

Sheehy, *Mas Sitigh:* Munster.

Tierney, *O Tighearnaigh:* 'lordly', Mayo, Donegal, Tipperary.

Tobin, de St Aubyn, *Tóibín:* Norman, Brittany, Munster.

Treacy, *O Treasigh:* 'fighter', Galway, Cork, Leix.

Tully, *O Taicligh:* 'peaceful', Connacht, Cavan, Longford, Westmeath.

Twomey, *O Tuama:* Cork, Kerry, Limerick.

Wall, de Valle, *du Val:* Norman, Carlow, Kilkenny, Waterford, Limerick, Cork.

Ward, *Mac an Bháird:* 'bard', Ulster, Connacht.

Woulfe, *de Bhulbh:* Norman, Kildare, Limerick, Cork.

List of Main Names
and Variants

Ahearne Hearne
    Ó hEachtighearna

Barry Barrymore
Beirne Ó Beirne
Blake Caddell
Boland Bolan Ó Beolláin
Boyle O Boyle Ó Baoighill
Browne Brown le Brun
Burke Bourke de Burgo
Butler
Byrne *see* O Byrne

Caddell *see* Blake
Cahill MacCathail
Carroll MacCarvill
    Ó Cearbhaill
Cavanagh *see* Kavanagh
Clarke *see* Clery
Clery Cleary Clarke
    Ó Cleirigh
Collins Ó Coileáin
Connolly Ó Conghaile
Cullen Ó Cuilin
Curtin MacCurtin Curtayne
    MacCuirtin
Curtayne *see* Curtin
Cusack Cíomhsóg

Daly Ó Dálaigh
Dillon
Doherty Ó Dochartaigh
Donoghue Dunphy
    Ó Donnchadha
Doyle Ó Dubhghaill
Duffy Ó Dubthaigh
Dunne Dunn Ó Duinn
Dunphy *see* Donoghue

Egan Keegan Mac-
    Aodhagáin

FitzGerald

Gallagher
    Ó Gallchobhair
Gilmartin *see* Martin
Guinness Magennis
    MacGuinness Mag
    Aonghusa

Hearne *see* Ahearne
Healy Hely Ó hEildhe
Hennessy Hensey
    Henchy O hAonghusa
Hensy *see* Hennessy
Henchy *see* Hennessy
Higgins Ó hUigín
Hoey *see* Keogh
Hogan Ó hÓgáin
Hoy *see* Keogh

Joyce

Kavanagh Cavanagh
    Caomhánach
Kane *see* Keane
Keane Kane Ó Catháin
Keegan *see* Egan
Kelly *see* O Kelly
Kennedy *see* O Kennedy
Keogh Kehoe Hoey Hoy
    Mac Eochaidh
Kehoe *see* Keogh
Kermode *see* MacDermot
Kirwan Ó Ciardubháin

Lacy de Lacy de Léis
Lynch Ó Loingsigh

MacCabe MacCába
MacCarthy MacCarthaigh
MacCarvill *see* Carroll
MacDermot MacDermott
    Kermode MacDiarmada
MacGrath Magraith Magraw
    MagRaith
MacGuinness *see* Guinness

94

Maguire MacGuire McGuire MagUidhir

MacKenna MacCionaoith

MacMahon Mohan Vaughan MacMathghamhna

Mohan *see* MacMahon

Malone Ó Maoileoin

Martin Martyn Gilmartin Ó Martain

Melia *see* O Malley

Moore Ó Mórdha

More O Ferrall *see* O Farrell

Mulryan *see* Ryan

Murphy O Morchoe

Nugent Nuinseann

O Brien

O Byrne Byrne Ó Broin

O Callaghan Ó Ceallacháin

O Connell Ó Conaill

O Connor O Conor Ó Conchobhair

O Donnell Ó Domhnaill

O Donovan Ó Donnabháin

O Farrell More O Ferrall Ó Fearghail

O Flaherty Ó Flaithbheartaigh

O Grady Ó Gradaigh

O Keeffe Ó Caoimh

O Kelly Ó Ceallaigh

O Kennedy Ó Cinnéide

O Mahony Ó Mahúna

O Malley Melia Ó Máille

O Neill

O Reilly Ó Raghailligh

O Rourke Ó Ruairc

O Sullivan Ó Súilcabháin

O Toole Ó Tuathail

Plunkett

Power de Paor

Regan Ó Ragáin

Roche de Róiste

Ryan Mulryan Ó Maoilriain

Sheridan Ó Sirideáin

Taaffe

Vaughan *see* MacMahon

Walsh Breathnach

The following names are illustrated on the front cover. Additional names on the cover illustration are listed in the text.

Artagan, Hartigan, *O hArtagáin:* formed from the first name Art, Clare, Limerick.

Bowe, Bowes, Bowie: anglicised from *O Buadhaigh,* meaning 'victorious', Cork.

O Bráonáin, Brennan: sorrow, Kerry, Kilkenny, Galway, Westmeath.

Cairbre, *Carbery,* O Cairbre: *cairbre* means 'charioteer', Waterford.

Dalton, D'Alton: Anglo-Norman, Meath, Westmeath, Clare.

Doheny, Dawney: anglicised from *I Dubhchanna,* meaning 'black Conna', Cork.

Goggin, Gogan, Cogan: Cork.

Hanley, Handly, *O hAinle:* from *áinle,* meaning 'beauty', Connacht, Cork.

McElligott, *MacEuileagóid:* Welsh-Norman, Kerry.

McGowan, *MacanGhabhann:* anglicised Smith, Cavan.